math expressions

Common Core

Dr. Karen C. Fuson

Watch the frog come alive in its pond as you discover and solve math challenges.

Download the *Math Worlds AR* app available on Android or iOS devices.

Grade 1

Volume 2

This material is based upon work supported by the

National Science Foundation
under Grant Numbers
ESI-9816320, REC-9806020, and RED-935373.

Any opinions, findings, and conclusions, or recommendations expressed in this material
are those of the author and do not necessarily reflect the views of the National Science Foundation.

P9-CCP-318

BIG IDEA 1 - Teen Solution Methods

Family Letter 201

Vocabulary Cards 202A

1 Unknown Partners with Teen Totals 203
  1.OA.A.1, 1.OA.C.5, 1.OA.C.6, 1.OA.D.8

  Purple Make-a-Ten Cards.. 203

2 Subtraction with Teen Numbers 209
  1.OA.A.1, 1.OA.B.4, 1.OA.C.5, 1.OA.C.6, 1.OA.D.8

  Blue Make-a-Ten Cards 209

3 Mixed Practice with Teen Problems 215
  1.OA.A.1, 1.OA.C.6, 1.OA.D.8

4 Small Group Practice with Teen Problems 217
  1.OA.A.1, 1.OA.B.3, 1.OA.C.5, 1.OA.C.6, 1.OA.D.8

5 Teen Problems with Various Unknowns.............................. 219
  1.OA.A.1, 1.OA.B.4, 1.OA.C.6, 1.OA.D.8

6 Problems with Three Addends.. 221
  1.OA.A.2, 1.OA.B.3

Quick Quiz 1 223

Fluency Check 11 224

BIG IDEA 2 - Find Patterns and Relationships

7 Count with Groups of 10.. 225
  1.NBT.A.1, 1.NBT.B.2

Family Letter 227

8 Numbers Through 120 229
  1.NBT.A.1, 1.NBT.B.2, 1.NBT.B.2.a, 1.NBT.B.2.b, 1.NBT.C.5

9 Add and Subtract Tens... 231
  1.NBT.A.1, 1.NBT.B.2, 1.NBT.C.4, 1.NBT.C.5, 1.NBT.C.6

10 Add and Subtract Multiples of 10 233
  1.OA.B.4, 1.OA.C.6, 1.OA.D.8, 1.NBT.B.2.a, 1.NBT.B.2.c, 1.NBT.C.4, 1.NBT.C.6

11 Focus on Mathematical Practices..................................... 235
  1.OA.A.1, 1.OA.A.2, 1.OA.C.6, 1.OA.D.7, 1.NBT.C.4, 1.NBT.C.6

Quick Quiz 2 237

Fluency Check 12 238

✓ UNIT 5 Review/Test 239

  Unit 5 Performance Task 243

BIG IDEA 1 - Represent and Compare Data

Family Letter 245

Vocabulary Cards 246A

1 Explore Representing Data.. 247
   1.OA.A.1, 1.OA.A.2, 1.MD.C.4

2 Organize Categorical Data 251
   1.OA.A.1, 1.MD.C.4

3 Use Stair Steps to Represent Data 253
   1.OA.A.1, 1.OA.C.6, 1.MD.C.4

4 Data Sets with Three Categories....................................... 255
   1.OA.A.1, 1.OA.A.2, 1.NBT.A.1, 1.MD.C.4

5 Data Collecting 257
   1.OA.A.1, 1.OA.A.2, 1.MD.C.4

Quick Quiz 1 259

Fluency Check 13 260

BIG IDEA 2 - *Compare* Problem Types

6 Introduce Comparison Bars 261
   1.OA.A.1, 1.OA.D.8

7 Comparison Bars and Comparing Language 263
   1.OA.A.1, 1.OA.D.8

8 Solve *Compare* Problems. 265
   1.OA.A.1, 1.OA.C.6

9 Focus on Mathematical Practices...................................... 267
   1.OA.A.1, 1.OA.A.2, 1.MD.C.4

Quick Quiz 2 269

Fluency Check 14 270

✓ UNIT 6 Review/Test 271

   Unit 6 Performance Task 275

BIG IDEA 1 - Tell and Write Time

Family Letter 277

Vocabulary Cards 280A

1 Introduction to Time 281
1.MD.B.3

2 Tell and Write Time in Hours 283
1.MD.B.3

   Student Clock 283

3 Time in Our Day 287
1.MD.B.3

   Clocks for "Our Busy Day" Book 287

4 Tell and Write Time in Half-Hours 291
1.MD.B.3

5 Practice Telling and Writing Time 293
1.OA.C.6, 1.MD.B.3

Quick Quiz 1 295

Fluency Check 15 296

BIG IDEA 2 - Shapes and Equal Shares

6 Squares and Other Rectangles 297
1.G.A.1

   2-Dimensional Shape Set 297

7 Triangles and Circles 303
1.G.A.1

8 Equal Shares 305
1.OA.C.6, 1.G.A.1, 1.G.A.3

   Equal Shares 305

9 Compose 2-Dimensional Shapes 309
1.G.A.1, 1.G.A.2, 1.G.A.3

   Inch Grid 309

   Triangle Grid 311

10 3-Dimensional Shapes 313
1.G.A.1, 1.G.A.2

11 Compose 3-Dimensional Shapes 315
1.G.A.2

Quick Quiz 2 317

Fluency Check 16 318

BIG IDEA 3 - Measure and Order by Length

12 Order by Length 319
  1.MD.A.1

13 Measure with Length Units 321
  1.MD.A.2, 1.OA.C.6

14 Focus on Mathematical Practices 323
  1.MD.A.1, 1.MD.A.2, 1.MD.B.3, 1.G.A.3

Quick Quiz 3 325

Fluency Check 17 326

☑ **UNIT 7 Review/Test** 327

  Unit 7 Performance Task 331

BIG IDEA - Add 2-Digit Numbers

Family Letter 333

1 Explore 2-Digit Addition 335
   1.NBT.B.2, 1.NBT.B.2.a, 1.NBT.B.2.c, 1.NBT.C.4

2 Methods of 2-Digit Addition 337
   1.NBT.C.4

3 Addition of Tens and Ones 339
   1.NBT.C.4

4 Discuss Solution Methods 341
   1.NBT.C.4

5 Practice 2-Digit Addition 343
   1.OA.C.6, 1.NBT.C.4

6 Focus on Mathematical Practices................................... 345
   1.NBT.B.3, 1.NBT.C.4, 1.NBT.C.6

Quick Quiz 1 347

Fluency Check 18 348

✓ UNIT 8 Review/Test 349

   Unit 8 Performance Task 353

Student Resources

Problem Types S1

Glossary S4

Correlation: Common Core State Standards for
Mathematical Content S17

Correlation: Common Core State Standards for
Mathematical Practice S21

Index.. S25

Dear Family:

In the previous unit, your child learned the Make a Ten strategy to find teen totals. Now, your child builds on previous knowledge to use make a ten to find an unknown partner. The Make a Ten strategy is explained below.

In a teen addition problem such as 9 + 5, children break apart the lesser number to make a ten with the greater number. Because 9 + 1 = 10, they break apart 5 into 1 + 4. Then they add the extra 4 onto 10 to find the total. A similar method is used to find unknown partners with teen totals. Children look for ways to make a ten because it is easier to add onto 10.

In the *Math Expressions* program, Make-a-Ten Cards help children use this method. Each card has a problem on the front. The back shows the answer and illustrates the Make a Ten strategy using pictures of dots. Below the pictures are corresponding numbers to help children understand how to make a ten. Practice the method with your child. As you continue to practice the Make a Ten strategy with your child, your child will become more adept at using mental math.

If you have any questions about the Make a Ten strategy, please contact me.

Sincerely,
Your child's teacher

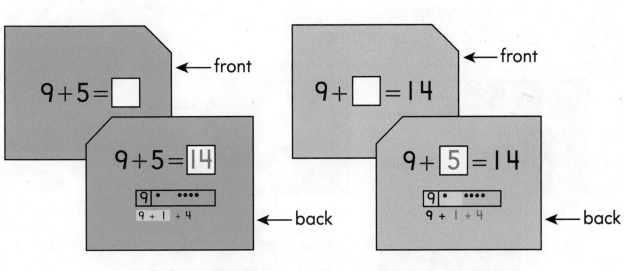

Make-a-Ten Cards

CC SS Unit 5 addresses the following standards from the Common Core State Standards for Mathematics: **1.OA.A.1, 1.OA.A.2, 1.OA.B.3, 1.OA.B.4, 1.OA.C.5, 1.OA.C.6, 1.OA.D.8, 1.NBT.A.1, 1.NBT.B.2, 1.NBT.B.2.c, 1.NBT.C.4, 1.NBT.C.5, 1.NBT.C.6,** and all Mathematical Practices.

Estimada familia:

En la unidad anterior, su niño aprendió la Estrategia hacer decenas para hallar totales de números de 11 a 19. Ahora, su niño ampliará esos conocimientos previos y hará decenas para hallar una parte desconocida. La Estrategia hacer decenas se explica debajo.

En una suma con números de 11 a 19, tal como $9 + 5$, los niños separan el número menor para formar una decena con el número mayor. Como $9 + 1 = 10$, separan el 5 en $1 + 4$. Luego suman al 10 los 4 que sobran para hallar el total. Un método semejante se usa para hallar partes desconocidas con totales de números de 11 a 19. Los niños buscan maneras de formar una decena porque es más fácil sumar con 10.

En el programa *Math Expressions* las tarjetas de hacer decenas ayudan a los niños a usar este método. Cada tarjeta tiene un problema en el frente. En el reverso se muestra la respuesta y se ilustra la Estrategia hacer decenas mediante dibujos de puntos. Debajo de los dibujos están los números correspondientes para ayudar a los niños a comprender cómo se hace una decena. Practique el método con su niño. A medida que practican la estrategia, su niño adquirirá mayor dominio del cálculo mental.

Si tiene alguna pregunta sobre la Estrategia hacer decenas, por favor comuníquese conmigo.

Atentamente,
El maestro de su niño

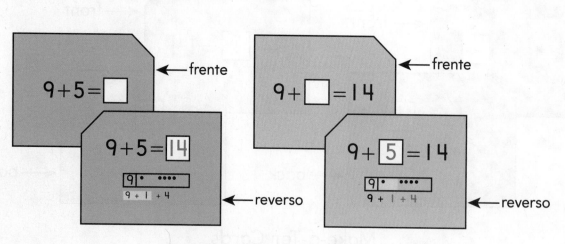

Tarjetas de hacer decenas

© Houghton Mifflin Harcourt Publishing Company

CC SS En la Unidad 5 se aplican los siguientes estándares de los Estándares estatales comunes de matemáticas: **1.OA.A.1, 1.OA.A.2, 1.OA.B.3, 1.OA.B.4, 1.OA.C.5, 1.OA.C.6, 1.OA.D.8, 1.NBT.A.1, 1.NBT.B.2, 1.NBT.B.2.c, 1.NBT.C.4, 1.NBT.C.5, 1.NBT.C.6 y todos los de** Prácticas matemáticas.

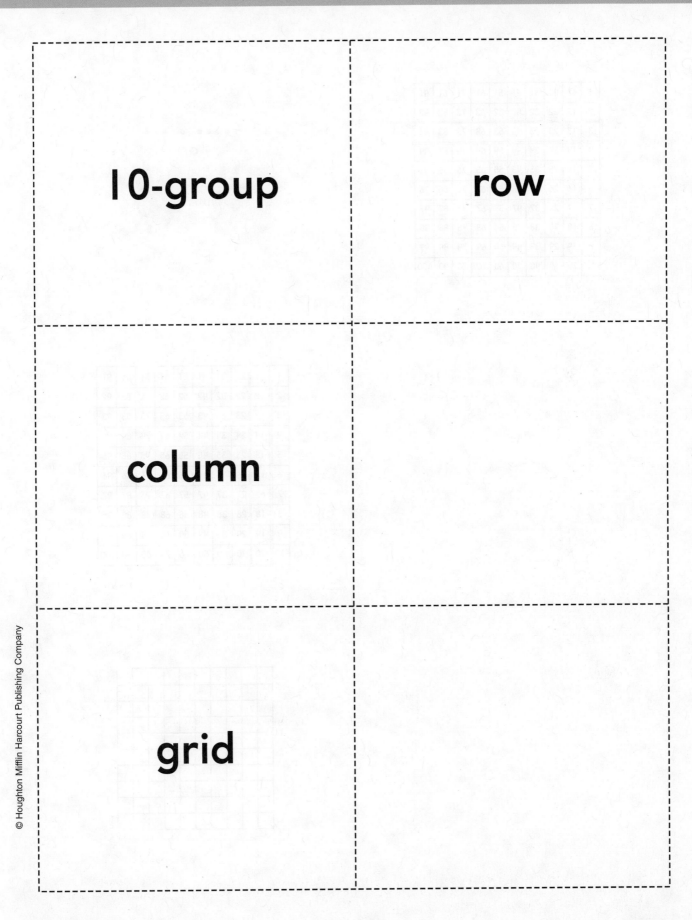

10-group

row

column

grid

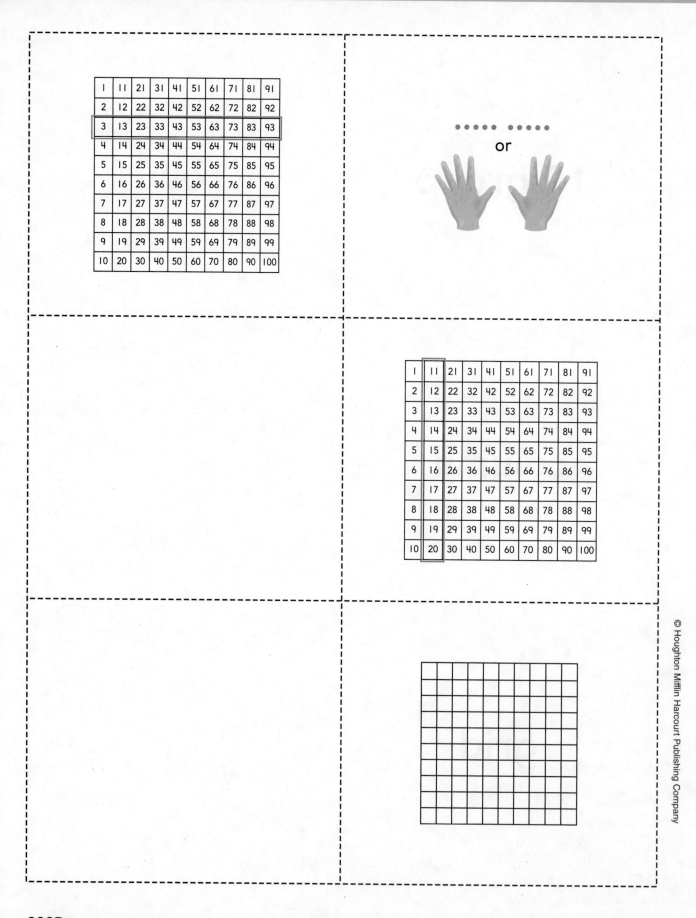

1	11	21	31	41	51	61	71	81	91
2	12	22	32	42	52	62	72	82	92
3	13	23	33	43	53	63	73	83	93
4	14	24	34	44	54	64	74	84	94
5	15	25	35	45	55	65	75	85	95
6	16	26	36	46	56	66	76	86	96
7	17	27	37	47	57	67	77	87	97
8	18	28	38	48	58	68	78	88	98
9	19	29	39	49	59	69	79	89	99
10	20	30	40	50	60	70	80	90	100

• • • • •   • • • • •

or

1	11	21	31	41	51	61	71	81	91
2	12	22	32	42	52	62	72	82	92
3	13	23	33	43	53	63	73	83	93
4	14	24	34	44	54	64	74	84	94
5	15	25	35	45	55	65	75	85	95
6	16	26	36	46	56	66	76	86	96
7	17	27	37	47	57	67	77	87	97
8	18	28	38	48	58	68	78	88	98
9	19	29	39	49	59	69	79	89	99
10	20	30	40	50	60	70	80	90	100

© Houghton Mifflin Harcourt Publishing Company

$7 + \boxed{} = 16$ $6 + \boxed{} = 15$ $7 + \boxed{} = 11$

$8 + \boxed{} = 12$ $9 + \boxed{} = 13$ $6 + \boxed{} = 11$

$7 + \boxed{} = 12$ $8 + \boxed{} = 13$ $9 + \boxed{} = 14$

$5 + \boxed{} = 11$ $9 + \boxed{} = 18$ $7 + \boxed{} = 13$

$8 + \boxed{} = 14$ $9 + \boxed{} = 15$ $4 + \boxed{} = 11$

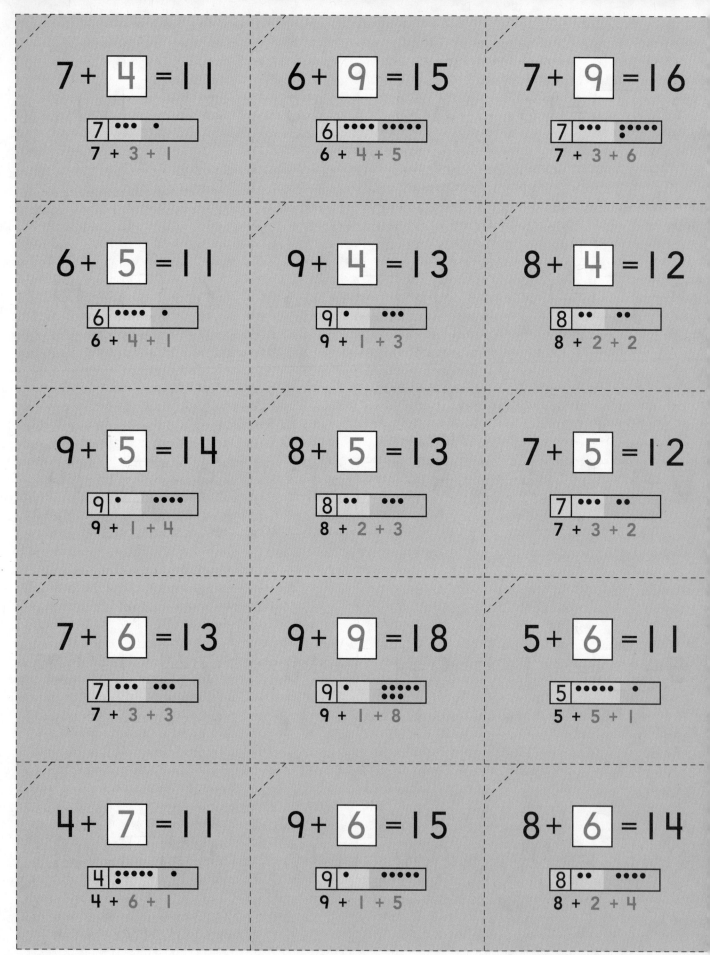

7 + 4 = 11

7 + 3 + 1

6 + 9 = 15

6 + 4 + 5

7 + 9 = 16

7 + 3 + 6

6 + 5 = 11

6 + 4 + 1

9 + 4 = 13

9 + 1 + 3

8 + 4 = 12

8 + 2 + 2

9 + 5 = 14

9 + 1 + 4

8 + 5 = 13

8 + 2 + 3

7 + 5 = 12

7 + 3 + 2

7 + 6 = 13

7 + 3 + 3

9 + 9 = 18

9 + 1 + 8

5 + 6 = 11

5 + 5 + 1

4 + 7 = 11

4 + 6 + 1

9 + 6 = 15

9 + 1 + 5

8 + 6 = 14

8 + 2 + 4

Purple Make-a-Ten Cards

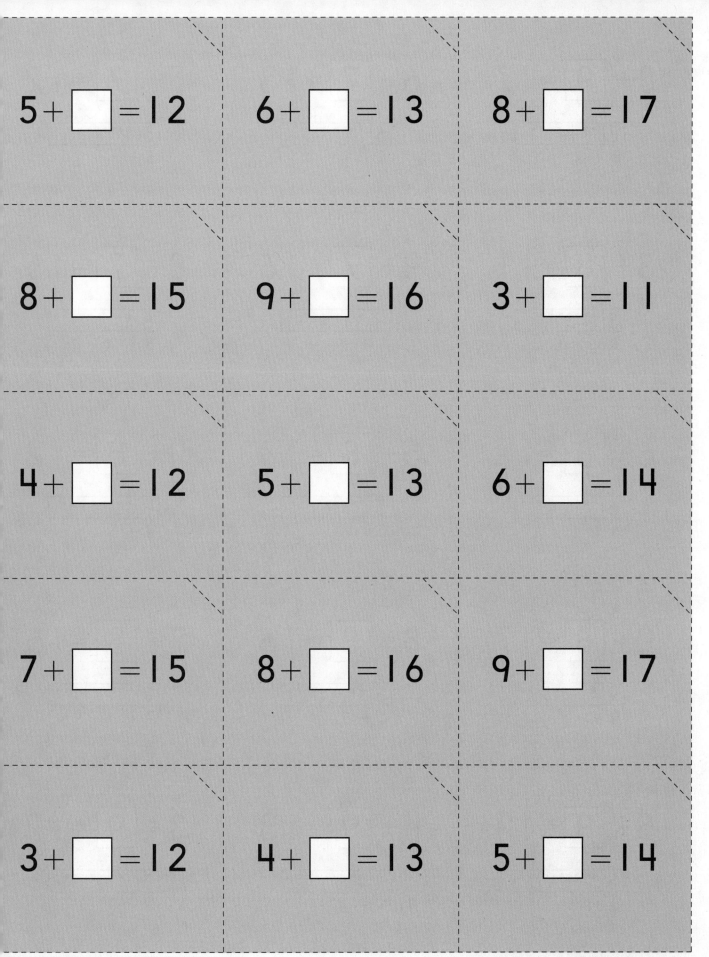

$5 + \boxed{} = 12$ $6 + \boxed{} = 13$ $8 + \boxed{} = 17$

$8 + \boxed{} = 15$ $9 + \boxed{} = 16$ $3 + \boxed{} = 11$

$4 + \boxed{} = 12$ $5 + \boxed{} = 13$ $6 + \boxed{} = 14$

$7 + \boxed{} = 15$ $8 + \boxed{} = 16$ $9 + \boxed{} = 17$

$3 + \boxed{} = 12$ $4 + \boxed{} = 13$ $5 + \boxed{} = 14$

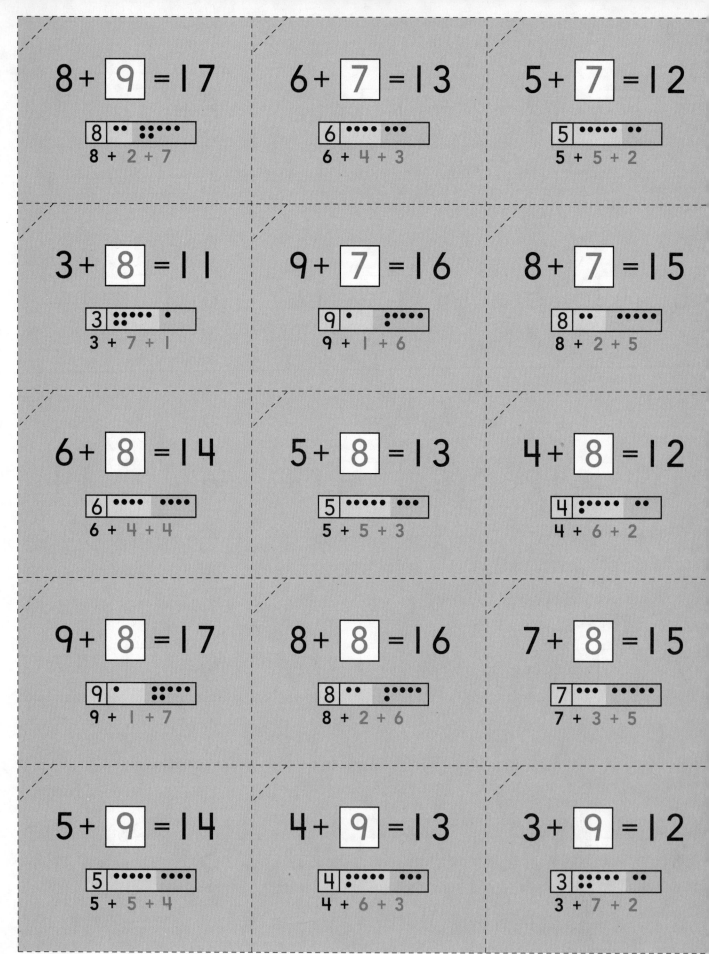

8 + [9] = 17
8 + 2 + 7

6 + [7] = 13
6 + 4 + 3

5 + [7] = 12
5 + 5 + 2

3 + [8] = 11
3 + 7 + 1

9 + [7] = 16
9 + 1 + 6

8 + [7] = 15
8 + 2 + 5

6 + [8] = 14
6 + 4 + 4

5 + [8] = 13
5 + 5 + 3

4 + [8] = 12
4 + 6 + 2

9 + [8] = 17
9 + 1 + 7

8 + [8] = 16
8 + 2 + 6

7 + [8] = 15
7 + 3 + 5

5 + [9] = 14
5 + 5 + 4

4 + [9] = 13
4 + 6 + 3

3 + [9] = 12
3 + 7 + 2

Purple Make-a-Ten Cards

Name _____

Match the equation with the picture that shows how to use the Make a Ten strategy to solve. Write the unknown partner.

1 $8 + \boxed{} = 12$

| 9 | •   • • |

2 $9 + \boxed{} = 15$

| 7 | • • •   • • |

3 $7 + \boxed{} = 12$

| 9 | •   • |

4 $8 + \boxed{} = 14$

| 8 | • •   • • |

5 $9 + \boxed{} = 12$

| 8 | • •   • • • • |

6 $8 + \boxed{} = 15$

| 9 | •   • • • • • |

7 $9 + \boxed{} = 11$

| 9 | •   • • • • • • • |

8 $9 + \boxed{} = 17$

| 8 | • •   • • • • • |

9 $7 + \boxed{} = 11$

| 7 | • • •   • |

CC SS Content Standards 1.OA.A.1, 1.OA.C.5, 1.OA.C.6, 1.OA.D.8
Mathematical Practices **MP2**

Solve the story problem.

Show your work.
Use drawings, numbers, or words.

---

10 Some birds are in a tree. 5 more birds fly into the tree. Now there are 13 birds. How many birds were in the tree before?

tree

☐ _____
label

---

11 14 cats are black or orange. 8 cats are black. How many cats are orange?

cat

☐ _____
label

---

12 10 kites are big. 10 kites are small. How many kites are there?

kite

☐ _____
label

---

13 Juan has 8 books. Meg brings more books. Now there are 17 books. How many books does Meg bring?

book

☐ _____
label

✓ **Check Understanding**

Listen. Then tell how to solve the story problem..

Unknown Partners with Teen Totals

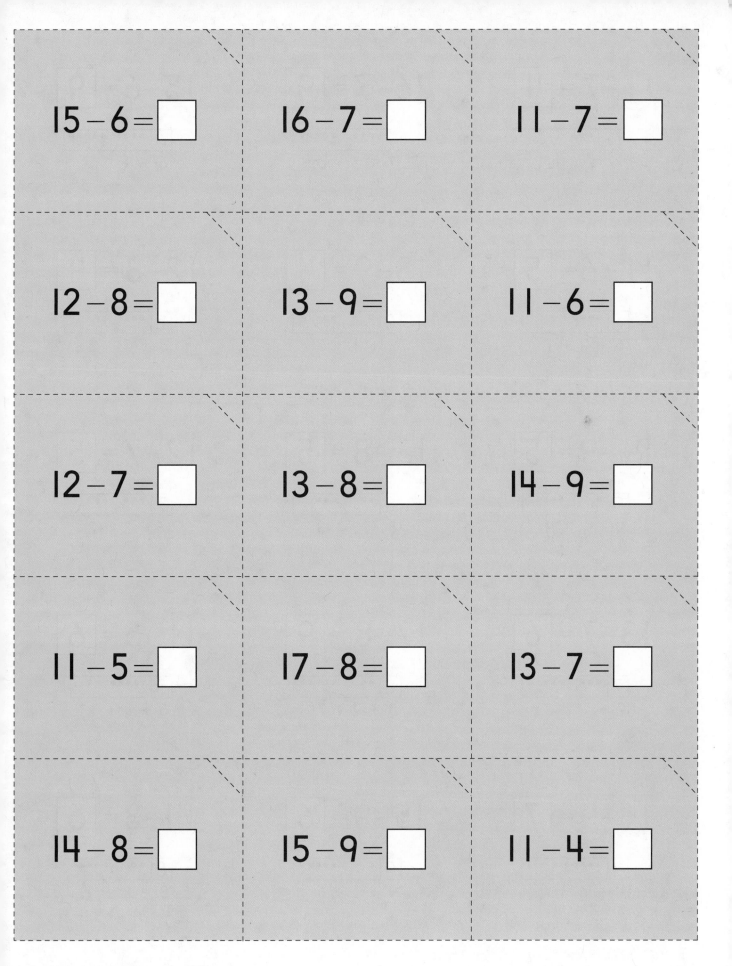

15 − 6 = ☐   16 − 7 = ☐   11 − 7 = ☐

12 − 8 = ☐   13 − 9 = ☐   11 − 6 = ☐

12 − 7 = ☐   13 − 8 = ☐   14 − 9 = ☐

11 − 5 = ☐   17 − 8 = ☐   13 − 7 = ☐

14 − 8 = ☐   15 − 9 = ☐   11 − 4 = ☐

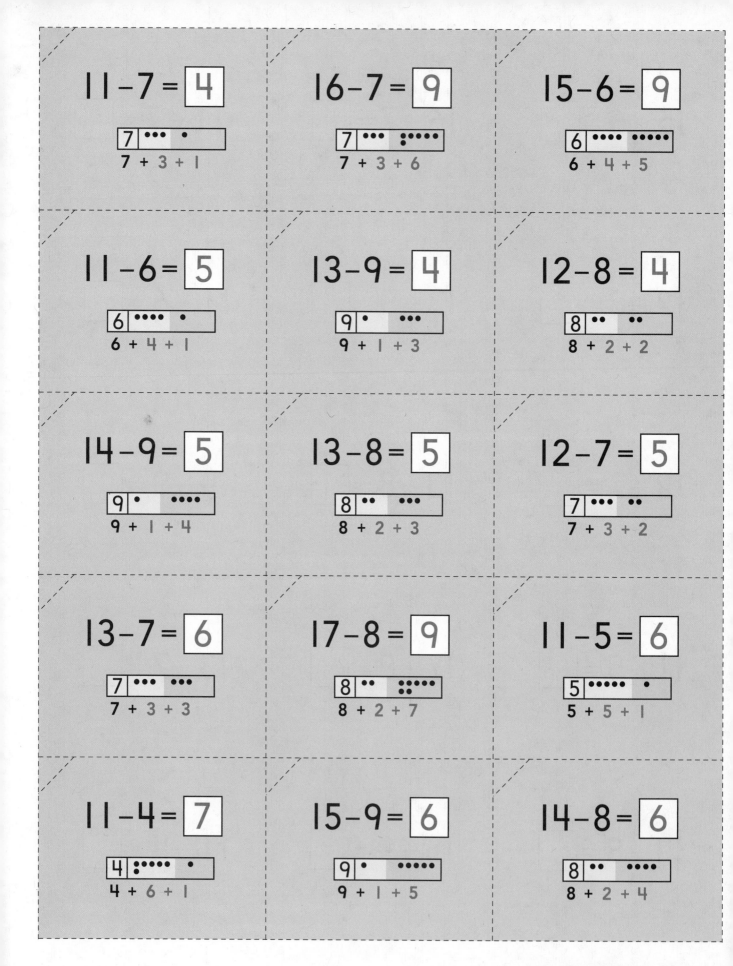

11 − 7 = 4
7 + 3 + 1

16 − 7 = 9
7 + 3 + 6

15 − 6 = 9
6 + 4 + 5

11 − 6 = 5
6 + 4 + 1

13 − 9 = 4
9 + 1 + 3

12 − 8 = 4
8 + 2 + 2

14 − 9 = 5
9 + 1 + 4

13 − 8 = 5
8 + 2 + 3

12 − 7 = 5
7 + 3 + 2

13 − 7 = 6
7 + 3 + 3

17 − 8 = 9
8 + 2 + 7

11 − 5 = 6
5 + 5 + 1

11 − 4 = 7
4 + 6 + 1

15 − 9 = 6
9 + 1 + 5

14 − 8 = 6
8 + 2 + 4

Blue Make-a-Ten Cards

$12 - 5 = \boxed{}$ $13 - 6 = \boxed{}$ $18 - 9 = \boxed{}$

$15 - 8 = \boxed{}$ $16 - 9 = \boxed{}$ $11 - 3 = \boxed{}$

$12 - 4 = \boxed{}$ $13 - 5 = \boxed{}$ $14 - 6 = \boxed{}$

$15 - 7 = \boxed{}$ $16 - 8 = \boxed{}$ $17 - 9 = \boxed{}$

$12 - 3 = \boxed{}$ $13 - 4 = \boxed{}$ $14 - 5 = \boxed{}$

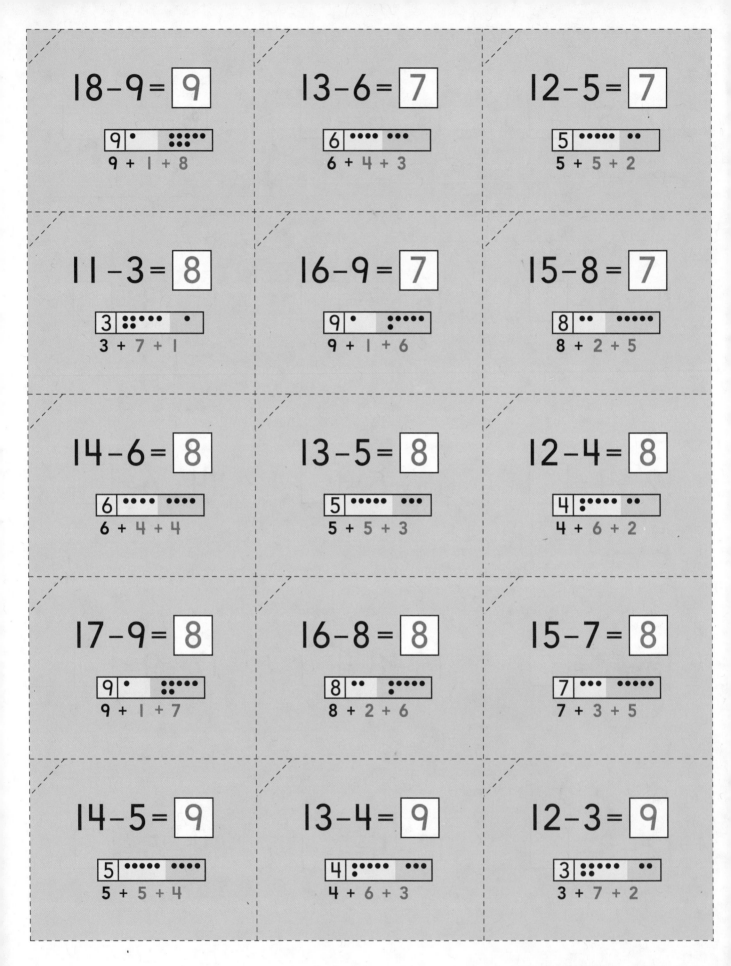

18 - 9 = 9
9 | · ····
9 + 1 + 8

13 - 6 = 7
6 | ···· ···
6 + 4 + 3

12 - 5 = 7
5 | ····· ··
5 + 5 + 2

11 - 3 = 8
3 | ··· ·
3 + 7 + 1

16 - 9 = 7
9 | · ·····
9 + 1 + 6

15 - 8 = 7
8 | ·· ·····
8 + 2 + 5

14 - 6 = 8
6 | ···· ····
6 + 4 + 4

13 - 5 = 8
5 | ····· ····
5 + 5 + 3

12 - 4 = 8
4 | ···· ··
4 + 6 + 2

17 - 9 = 8
9 | · ·····
9 + 1 + 7

16 - 8 = 8
8 | ·· ······
8 + 2 + 6

15 - 7 = 8
7 | ··· ·····
7 + 3 + 5

14 - 5 = 9
5 | ····· ····
5 + 5 + 4

13 - 4 = 9
4 | ···· ···
4 + 6 + 3

12 - 3 = 9
3 | ··· ··
3 + 7 + 2

Blue Make-a-Ten Cards

Match the equation with the picture that shows
how to use the Make a Ten strategy to solve.

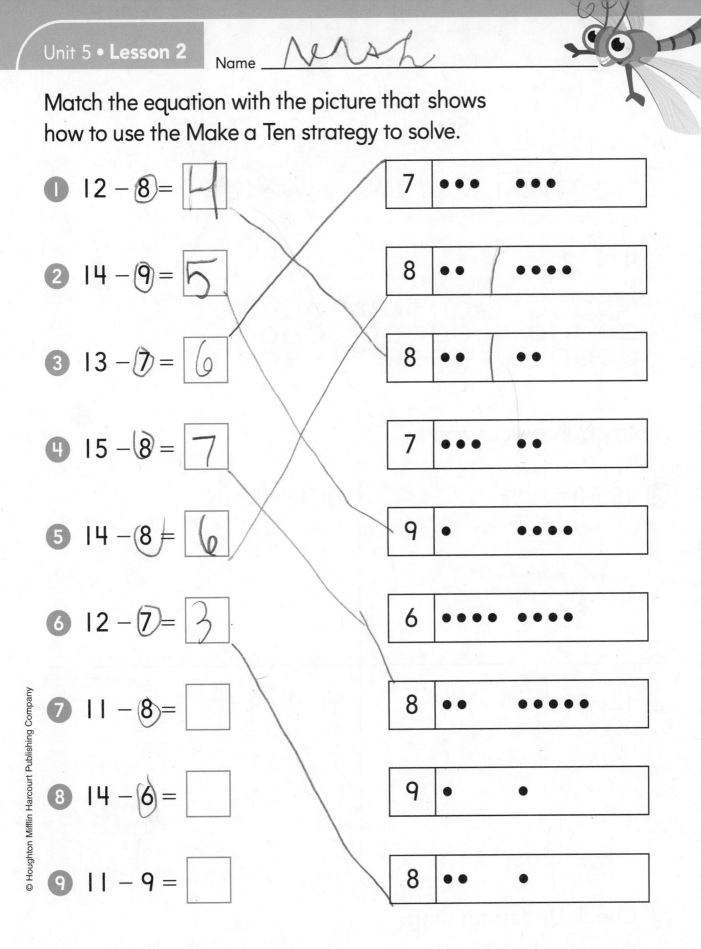

1. $12 - 8 = 4$

2. $14 - 9 = 5$

3. $13 - 7 = 6$

4. $15 - 8 = 7$

5. $14 - 8 = 6$

6. $12 - 7 = 3$

7. $11 - 8 =$ ☐

8. $14 - 6 =$ ☐

9. $11 - 9 =$ ☐

7	••• •••
8	•• ••••
8	•• ••
7	••• ••
9	• ••••
6	•••• ••••
8	•• •••••
9	• •
8	•• •

© Houghton Mifflin Harcourt Publishing Company

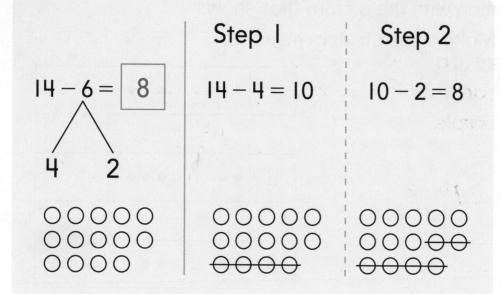

14 − 6 = 8	Step 1	Step 2
4 2	14 − 4 = 10	10 − 2 = 8

Subtract. Show your work.

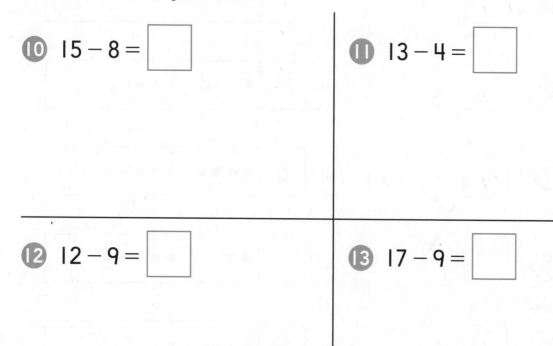

⑩ 15 − 8 = ☐

⑪ 13 − 4 = ☐

⑫ 12 − 9 = ☐

⑬ 17 − 9 = ☐

✔ **Check Understanding**

Draw to show how to make a ten to solve 13 − 8.

Subtraction with Teen Numbers

Name _____

Solve the story problem.   Show your work.
                            Use drawings, numbers, or words.

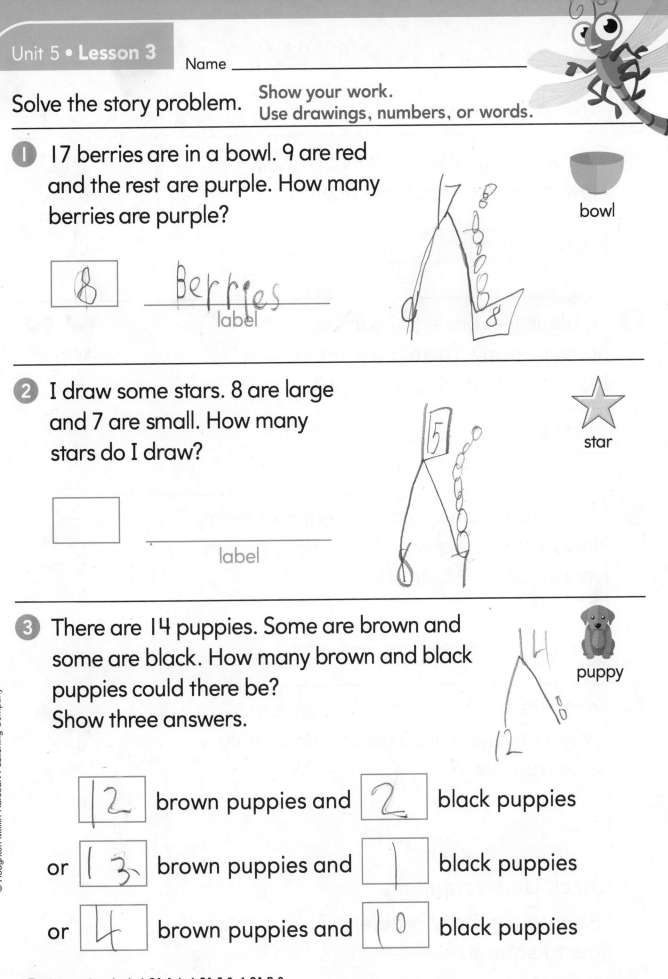

1 17 berries are in a bowl. 9 are red and the rest are purple. How many berries are purple?

| 8 |

Berries
label

bowl

2 I draw some stars. 8 are large and 7 are small. How many stars do I draw?

| |

label

star

3 There are 14 puppies. Some are brown and some are black. How many brown and black puppies could there be?
Show three answers.

puppy

| 12 | brown puppies and | 2 | black puppies

or | 13 | brown puppies and | 1 | black puppies

or | 4 | brown puppies and | 10 | black puppies

Solve the story problem.

Show your work.
Use drawings, numbers, or words.

4 15 frogs are by the pond. 9 hop away. How many frogs are there now?

$15 - 9 = 6$

6

frogs
label

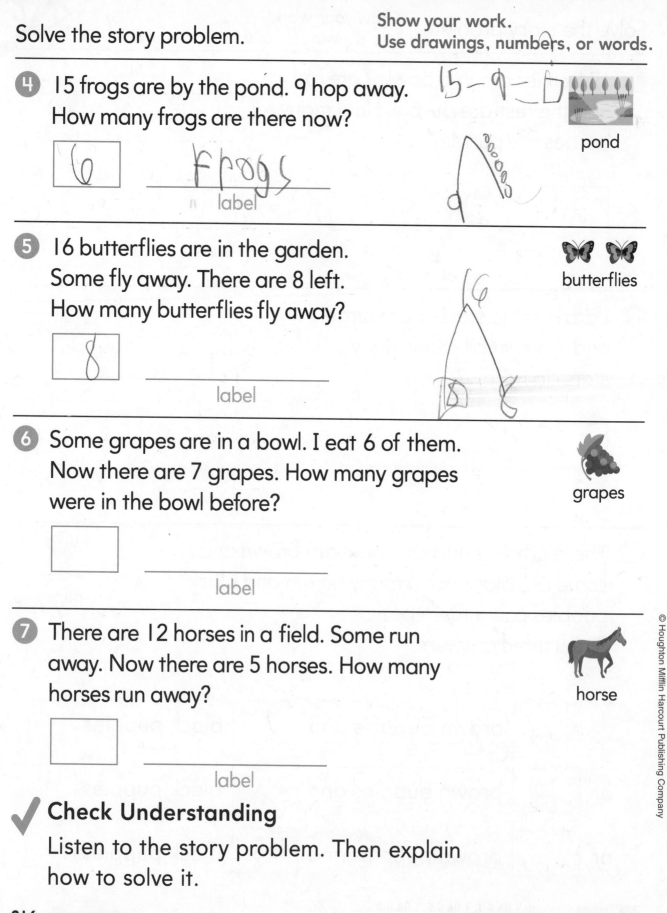

pond

5 16 butterflies are in the garden. Some fly away. There are 8 left. How many butterflies fly away?

8

label

butterflies

6 Some grapes are in a bowl. I eat 6 of them. Now there are 7 grapes. How many grapes were in the bowl before?

label

grapes

7 There are 12 horses in a field. Some run away. Now there are 5 horses. How many horses run away?

label

horse

✓ **Check Understanding**

Listen to the story problem. Then explain how to solve it.

Mixed Practice with Teen Problems

Name _____

Match the equation with the picture that shows how to use the Make a Ten strategy to solve.

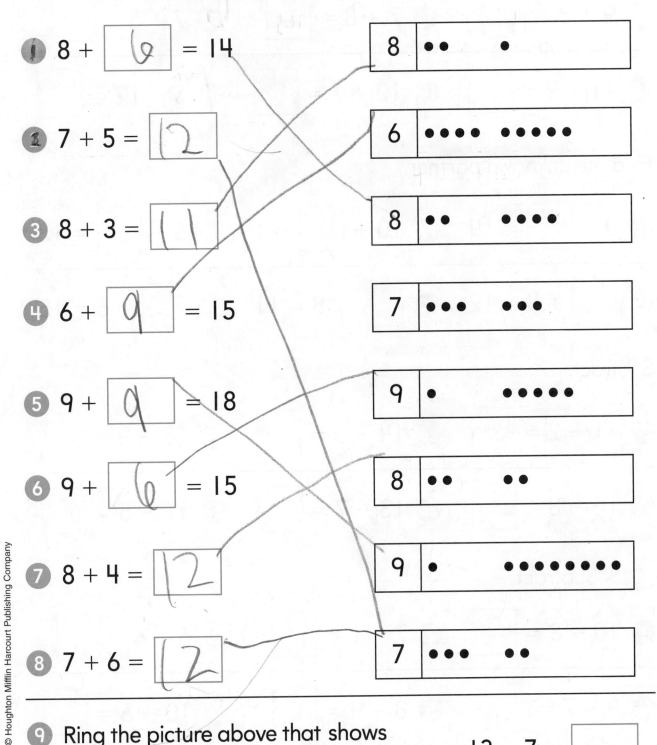

1 $8 + \boxed{6} = 14$ | 8 | ••   • |

2 $7 + 5 = \boxed{12}$ | 6 | •••• ••••• |

3 $8 + 3 = \boxed{11}$ | 8 | ••   •••• |

4 $6 + \boxed{9} = 15$ | 7 | •••   ••• |

5 $9 + \boxed{9} = 18$ | 9 | •   ••••• |

6 $9 + \boxed{6} = 15$ | 8 | ••   •• |

7 $8 + 4 = \boxed{12}$ | 9 | •   •••••••• |

8 $7 + 6 = \boxed{12}$ | 7 | •••   •• |

9 Ring the picture above that shows how to use the Make a Ten strategy to solve the equation.

$13 - 7 = \boxed{}$

© Houghton Mifflin Harcourt Publishing Company

Add.

10 $9 + 3 = \boxed{12}$ **11** $7 + 8 = \boxed{14}$ **12** $7 + 5 = \boxed{}$

13 $11 + 9 = \boxed{}$ **14** $12 + 7 = \boxed{}$ **15** $8 + 12 = \boxed{}$

Find the unknown partner.

16 $9 + \boxed{} = 14$ **17** $10 + \boxed{} = 19$ **18** $6 + \boxed{} = 13$

19 $\boxed{} + 4 = 12$ **20** $\boxed{} + 8 = 11$ **21** $\boxed{} + 6 = 15$

Subtract.

22 $11 - 2 = \boxed{}$ **23** $14 - 6 = \boxed{}$ **24** $13 - 9 = \boxed{}$

25 $16 - 8 = \boxed{}$ **26** $13 - 7 = \boxed{}$ **27** $12 - 5 = \boxed{}$

PATH to FLUENCY Subtract.

1 $10 - 8 = \boxed{}$ **2** $7 - 1 = \boxed{}$ **3** $6 - 6 = \boxed{}$

4 $9 - 7 = \boxed{}$ **5** $8 - 4 = \boxed{}$ **6** $10 - 6 = \boxed{}$

✓ **Check Understanding**

Explain how to make ten to solve. $17 - 8 = \boxed{}$

    Small Group Practice with Teen Problems

Name _____

1 Rosa reads 8 stories. Tim reads 5 stories.
How many stories do they read in all?

2 Rosa reads 8 stories. Tim also reads some stories.
They read 13 stories in all. How many stories
does Tim read?

8 000000

3 Rosa reads some stories. Tim reads 5 stories. They read 13
stories in all. How many stories does Rosa read?

CC SS Content Standards 1.OA.A.1, 1.OA.B.4, 1.OA.C.6, 1.OA.D.8
Mathematical Practices MP2, MP3, MP6, MP7

Some crayons are in a box.
I take 6 crayons out.
Now there are 9 crayons in the box.
How many crayons were in the box before?

Am I correct?

4 Look at what Puzzled Penguin wrote.

| 9 | – | 6 | = | 3 |

| 3 | crayons

5 Help Puzzled Penguin.

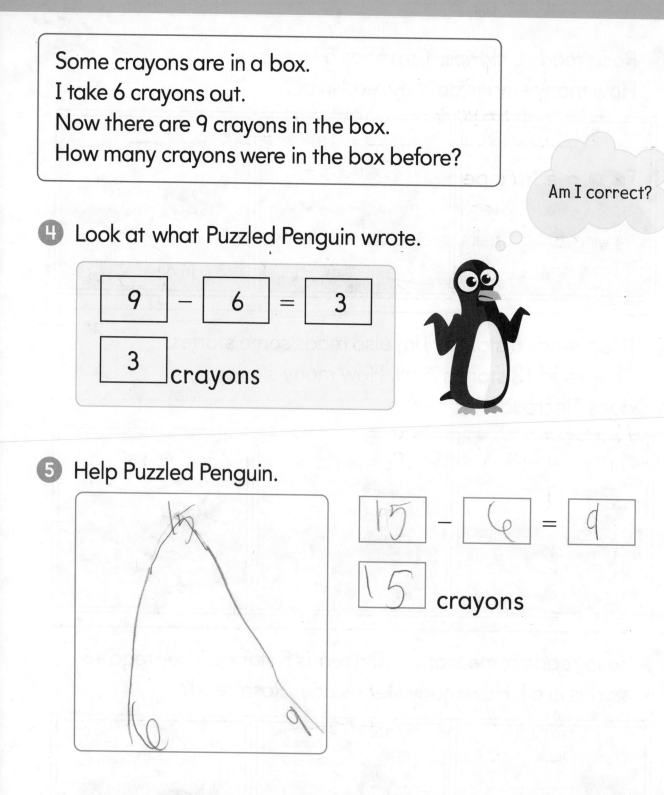

| 15 | – | 6 | = | 9 |

| 15 | crayons

✓ **Check Understanding**

Make up a story problem to find the unknown total and another story problem to find an unknown partner.

Teen Problems with Various Unknowns

Name _____

Model and solve the story problem.
Color to show your model.
Cross out the cubes you do not use.

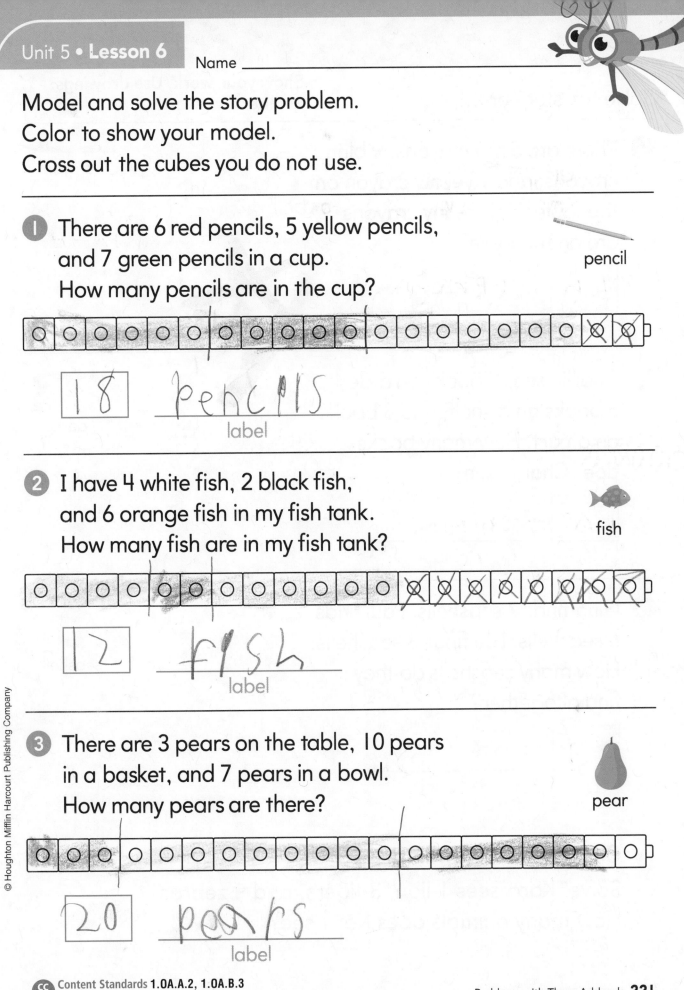

1 There are 6 red pencils, 5 yellow pencils,
and 7 green pencils in a cup.
How many pencils are in the cup?

pencil

18   pencils
      label

2 I have 4 white fish, 2 black fish,
and 6 orange fish in my fish tank.
How many fish are in my fish tank?

fish

12   fish
      label

3 There are 3 pears on the table, 10 pears
in a basket, and 7 pears in a bowl.
How many pears are there?

pear

20   pears
      label

© Houghton Mifflin Harcourt Publishing Company

Solve the story problem.

Show your work. Use drawings, numbers, or words.

4 There are 5 red crayons, 9 blue crayons, and 1 yellow crayon on the table. How many crayons are on the table?

crayon

| 15 | Crayons |

label

5 Charlie sees 4 books on a desk, 6 books on a shelf, and 8 books on a cart. How many books does Charlie see?

desk

| 18 | books |

label

6 Gina finds 7 seashells. Paul finds 6 seashells. Lee finds 3 seashells. How many seashells do they find altogether?

seashell

| 16 | seashells |

label

✓ **Check Understanding**

Solve. Kara sees 1 lion, 3 tigers, and 9 zebras. How many animals does Kara see?

Problems with Three Addends

I Ring **10-groups**. Count by tens and ones.
Write the number.

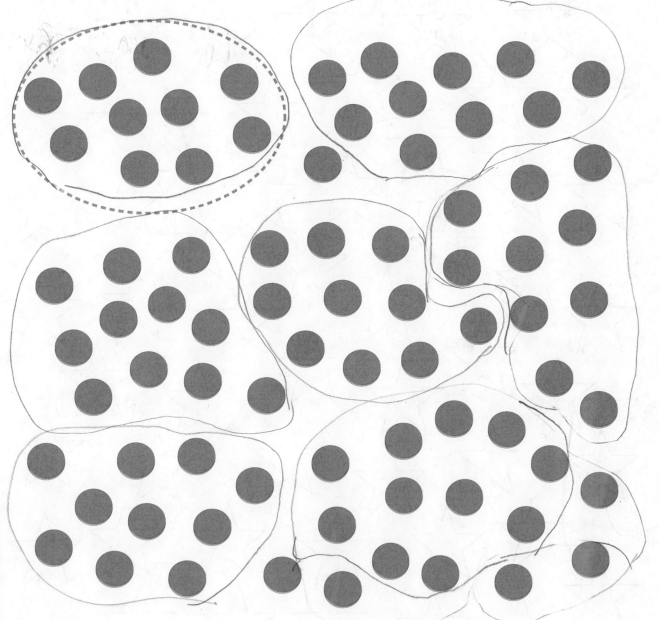

2 Color each 10-group a different color.
Count by tens and ones. Write the number.

✓ **Check Understanding**

Explain how to use tens and ones to
count 95 counters.

Count with Groups of 10

Dear Family:

The next several lessons of this unit build upon what the class learned previously about tens and ones. The Hundred Grid is a tool that allows children to see 10-based patterns in sequence. Seeing numbers in the ordered rows and columns of the Hundred Grid helps children better understand number relationships as they:

- continue to practice with 10-groups, adding tens to any 2-digit number, with totals to 100;
- explore 2-digit subtraction, subtracting tens from decade numbers;
- connect what they know about 10-partners to now find 100-partners.

1	11	21	31	41	51	61	71	81	91
2	12	22	32	42	52	62	72	82	92
3	13	23	33	43	53	63	73	83	93
4	14	24	34	44	54	64	74	84	94
5	15	25	35	45	55	65	75	85	95
6	16	26	36	46	56	66	76	86	96
7	17	27	37	47	57	67	77	87	97
8	18	28	38	48	58	68	78	88	98
9	19	29	39	49	59	69	79	89	99
10	20	30	40	50	60	70	80	90	100

3 ooo
13 | ooo
23 || ooo
33 ||| ooo
43 |||| ooo
53 ||||| ooo
63 ||||| | ooo
73 ||||| || ooo
83 ||||| ||| ooo
93 ||||| |||| ooo

If you have any questions or problems, please contact me.

Sincerely,
Your child's teacher

CC SS Unit 5 addresses the following standards from the Common Core State Standards for Mathematics: **1.OA.A.1, 1.OA.A.2, 1.OA.B.3, 1.OA.B.4, 1.OA.C.5, 1.OA.C.6, 1.OA.D.8, 1.NBT.A.1, 1.NBT.B.2, 1.NBT.B.2.a, 1.NBT.B.2.b, 1.NBT.B.2.c, 1.NBT.C.4, 1.NBT.C.5, 1.NBT.C.6,** and all Mathematical Practices.

Estimada familia:

Las siguientes lecciones en esta unidad amplían lo que la clase aprendió anteriormente acerca de decenas y unidades. La Cuadrícula de 100 es un instrumento que permite observar patrones de base 10 en secuencia. Observar los números ordenados en hileras y columnas en la Cuadrícula de 100 ayudará a los niños a comprender mejor la relación entre los números mientras:

- continúan practicando con grupos de 10, sumando decenas a números de 2 dígitos con totales hasta 100;

- exploran la resta de números de 2 dígitos, restando decenas de números que terminan en cero;

- relacionan lo que saben acerca de las partes de 10 para hallar partes de 100.

1	11	21	31	41	51	61	71	81	91
2	12	22	32	42	52	62	72	82	92
3	13	23	33	43	53	63	73	83	93
4	14	24	34	44	54	64	74	84	94
5	15	25	35	45	55	65	75	85	95
6	16	26	36	46	56	66	76	86	96
7	17	27	37	47	57	67	77	87	97
8	18	28	38	48	58	68	78	88	98
9	19	29	39	49	59	69	79	89	99
10	20	30	40	50	60	70	80	90	100

3 ∘∘∘

13 | ∘∘∘

23 | | ∘∘∘

33 | | | ∘∘∘

43 | | | | ∘∘∘

53 | | | | | ∘∘∘

63 | | | | | | ∘∘∘

73 | | | | | | | ∘∘∘

83 | | | | | | | | ∘∘∘

93 | | | | | | | | | ∘∘∘

Si tiene alguna pregunta o algún comentario comuníquese conmigo.

Atentamente,
El maestro de su niño

En la Unidad 5 se aplican los siguientes estándares de los Estándares estatales comunes de matemáticas: 1.OA.A.1, 1.OA.A.2, 1.OA.B.3, 1.OA.B.4, 1.OA.C.5, 1.OA.C.6, 1.OA.D.8, 1.NBT.A.1, 1.NBT.B.2, 1.NBT.B.2.a, 1.NBT.B.2.b, 1.NBT.B.2.c, 1.NBT.C.4, 1.NBT.C.5, 1.NBT.C.6 y todos los de Prácticas matemáticas.

Name _____

VOCABULARY
column
grid

1 Write the numbers 1–120 in **columns**.

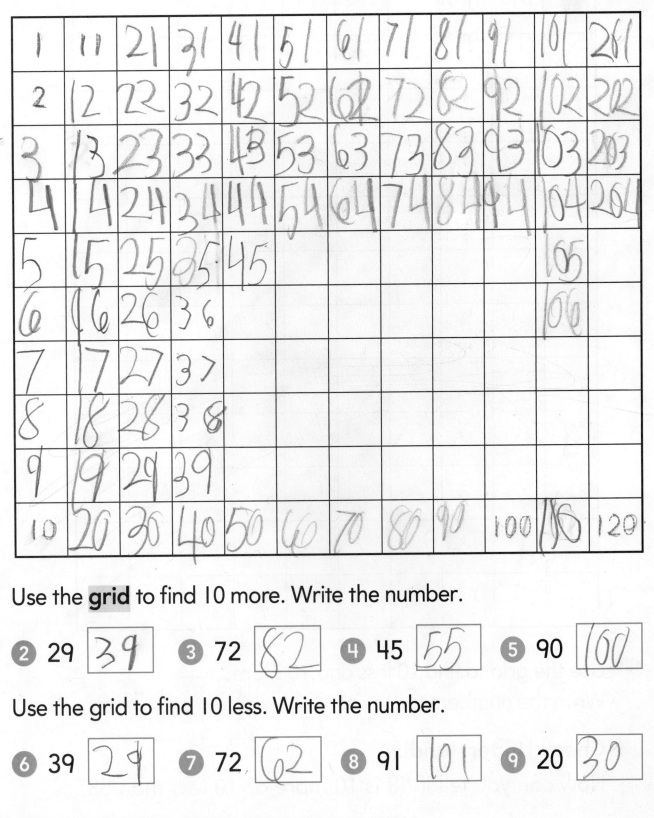

1	11	21	31	41	51	61	71	81	91	101	211
2	12	22	32	42	52	62	72	82	92	102	212
3	13	23	33	43	53	63	73	83	93	103	203
4	14	24	34	44	54	64	74	84	94	104	204
5	15	25	35	45						105	
6	16	26	36							106	
7	17	27	37								
8	18	28	38								
9	19	29	39								
10	20	30	40	50	60	70	80	90	100	110	120

Use the **grid** to find 10 more. Write the number.

2 29 [39]   **3** 72 [82]   **4** 45 [55]   **5** 90 [100]

Use the grid to find 10 less. Write the number.

6 39 [29]   **7** 72 [62]   **8** 91 [101]   **9** 20 [30]

CC SS Content Standards 1.NBT.A.1, 1.NBT.B.2, 1.NBT.B.2.a, 1.NBT.B.2.b, 1.NBT.C.5
Mathematical Practices MP5, MP6, MP7, MP8

Numbers Through 120 **229**

10 Write the numbers 1–120 in **rows**.

VOCABULARY
row

1	2	3							10
11									
									100
									120

11 Use the grid to find 10 less and 10 more.
Write the numbers.

41 51 61

✔ **Check Understanding**

How can you tell if 48 is 10 more or 10 less than 58?

© Houghton Mifflin Harcourt Publishing Company

Numbers Through 120

Name _____

1 Listen to the directions.

1	11	21	31	41	51	61	71	81	91
2	12	22	32	42	52	62	72	82	92
3	13	23	33	43	53	63	73	83	93
4	14	24	34	44	54	64	74	84	94
5	15	25	35	45	55	65	75	85	95
6	16	26	36	46	56	66	76	86	96
7	17	27	37	47	57	67	77	87	97
8	18	28	38	48	58	68	78	88	98
9	19	29	39	49	59	69	79	89	99
10	20	30	40	50	60	70	80	90	100

CCSS Content Standards **1.NBT.A.1, 1.NBT.B.2, 1.NBT.C.4, 1.NBT.C.5, 1.NBT.C.6**
Mathematical Practices **MP5, MP6**

Add and Subtract Tens **231**

Add tens.

2 89 + 10 = 99

3 43 + 20 = 63

4 28 + 50 = 68

5 32 + 40 = 72

6 11 + 20 = 31

7 42 + 30 = 62

8 52 + 40 = 92

9 12 + 40 = 52

Subtract tens.

10 30 − 20 = 10

11 60 − 10 = 50

12 70 − 40 = 30

13 70 − 20 = 50

14 90 − 60 = 30

15 80 − 70 = 10

16 90 − 10 = 80

17 50 − 40 = 10

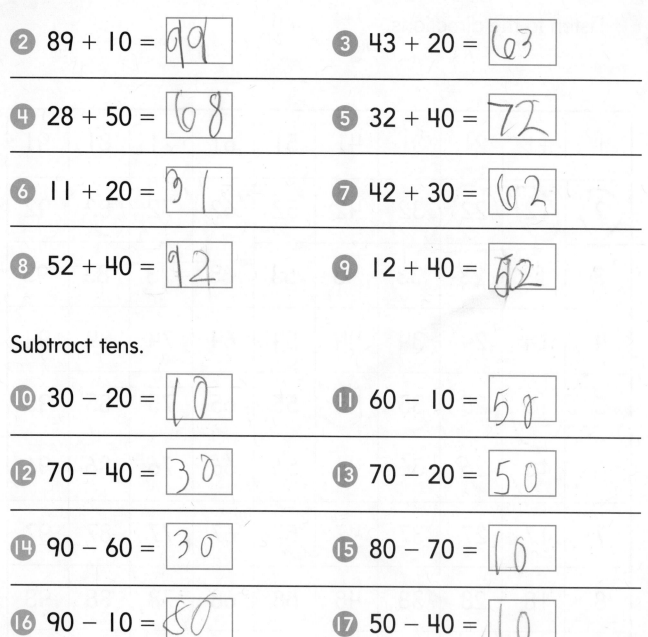

✓ Check Understanding

Write an equation to solve each problem.

Add 4 tens to 35.　　　　Subtract 6 tens from 9 tens.

© Houghton Mifflin Harcourt Publishing Company

　　　　Add and Subtract Tens

Name _____

Solve.

① $80 + 20 = \boxed{100}$

② $30 + 70 = \boxed{100}$

③ $10 + \boxed{90} = 100$

④ $50 + \boxed{50} = 100$

⑤ $100 = 20 + \boxed{50}$

⑥ $100 = 40 + \boxed{60}$

⑦ $20 + 50 = \boxed{70}$

⑧ $10 + 80 = \boxed{90}$

⑨ $0 + 60 = \boxed{60}$

⑩ $20 + 20 = \boxed{40}$

⑪ $40 - 40 = \boxed{0}$

⑫ $80 - 0 = \boxed{80}$

⑬ $70 - 60 = \boxed{10}$

⑭ $60 - 30 = \boxed{90}$

⑮ $60 - 10 = \boxed{50}$

⑯ $70 - 40 = \boxed{30}$

$10 + \boxed{50} = 60$

$40 + \boxed{30} = 70$

⑰ $50 - 20 = \boxed{30}$

⑱ $90 - 50 = \boxed{40}$

$20 + \boxed{30} = 50$

$50 + \boxed{40} = 90$

CC SS Content Standards **1.OA.C.6, 1.NBT.C.4, 1.NBT.C.6**
Mathematical Practices **MP3, MP6, MP7**

19 Look at what Puzzled Penguin wrote.

70 − 20 = | 5 |

Am I correct?

20 Help Puzzled Penguin.

TXIIIII

70 − 20 = | 50 |

PATH to FLUENCY Add.

1 1 + 8 = | 9 | **2** 5 + 4 = | 9 | **3** 4 + 6 = | 10 |

PATH to FLUENCY Subtract.

4 9 − 3 = | 6 | **5** 6 − 1 = | 5 | **6** 7 − 6 = | 1 |

✓ **Check Understanding**
Add and subtract tens.

60 + 40 = | 100 | 60 − 40 = | 20 |

Add and Subtract Multiples of 10

Use the picture.
Write the numbers to solve.

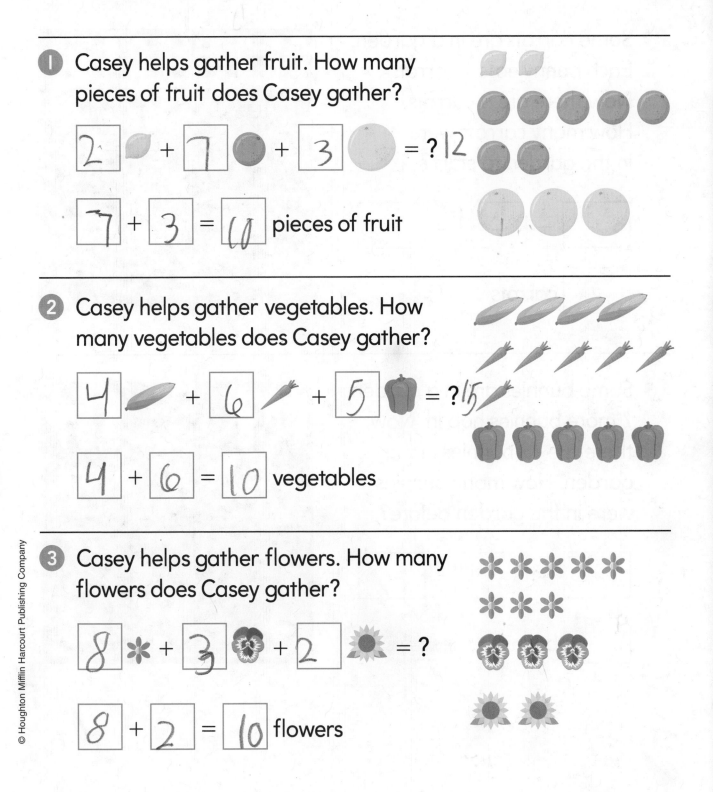

1   Casey helps gather fruit. How many
    pieces of fruit does Casey gather?

    $\boxed{2}$ 🍋 + $\boxed{7}$ 🔴 + $\boxed{3}$ ⚪ = ? 12

    $\boxed{7}$ + $\boxed{3}$ = $\boxed{10}$ pieces of fruit

2   Casey helps gather vegetables. How
    many vegetables does Casey gather?

    $\boxed{4}$ 🌽 + $\boxed{6}$ 🥕 + $\boxed{5}$ 🫑 = ? 15

    $\boxed{4}$ + $\boxed{6}$ = $\boxed{10}$ vegetables

3   Casey helps gather flowers. How many
    flowers does Casey gather?

    $\boxed{8}$ ✽ + $\boxed{3}$ 🌸 + $\boxed{2}$ 🌼 = ?

    $\boxed{8}$ + $\boxed{2}$ = $\boxed{10}$ flowers

Use the picture.
Write the numbers to solve.

4 Some carrots are in a garden.
Each bunny eats 1 carrot.
Now there are 9 carrots.
How many carrots were
in the garden to start?

$$\boxed{14} - \boxed{5} = \boxed{9}$$

$\boxed{9}$ carrots

---

5 Some bunnies are in a garden.
7 more bunnies hop in. Now
there are 13 bunnies in the
garden. How many bunnies
were in the garden before?

$$\boxed{} + \boxed{} = \boxed{}$$

$\boxed{}$ bunnies

Focus on Mathematical Practices

Name ______________________ Date ______________

Use the grid.

51	52	53	54	55	56	57	58	59	60
61	62	63	64	65	66	67	68	69	70
71	72	73	74	75	76	77	78	79	80

1. 10 more than 54 is [64].

2. 10 more than 68 is [78].

Add or subtract tens.

3. 68 + 30 = [98]

4. 52 + 20 = [72]

5. 80 − 50 = [30]

Name _____   Date _____

Add.

1 $3 + 3 =$ ☐   2 $6 + 1 =$ ☐   3 $4 + 2 =$ ☐

4 $3 + 4 =$ ☐   5 $6 + 2 =$ ☐   6 $5 + 4 =$ ☐

Subtract.

7 $6 - 4 =$ ☐   8 $8 - 5 =$ ☐   9 $7 - 3 =$ ☐

10 $8 - 6 =$ ☐   11 $9 - 2 =$ ☐   12 $7 - 1 =$ ☐

13 $10 - 10 =$ ☐   14 $10 - 7 =$ ☐   15 $9 - 8 =$ ☐

Match the box to the unknown partner.

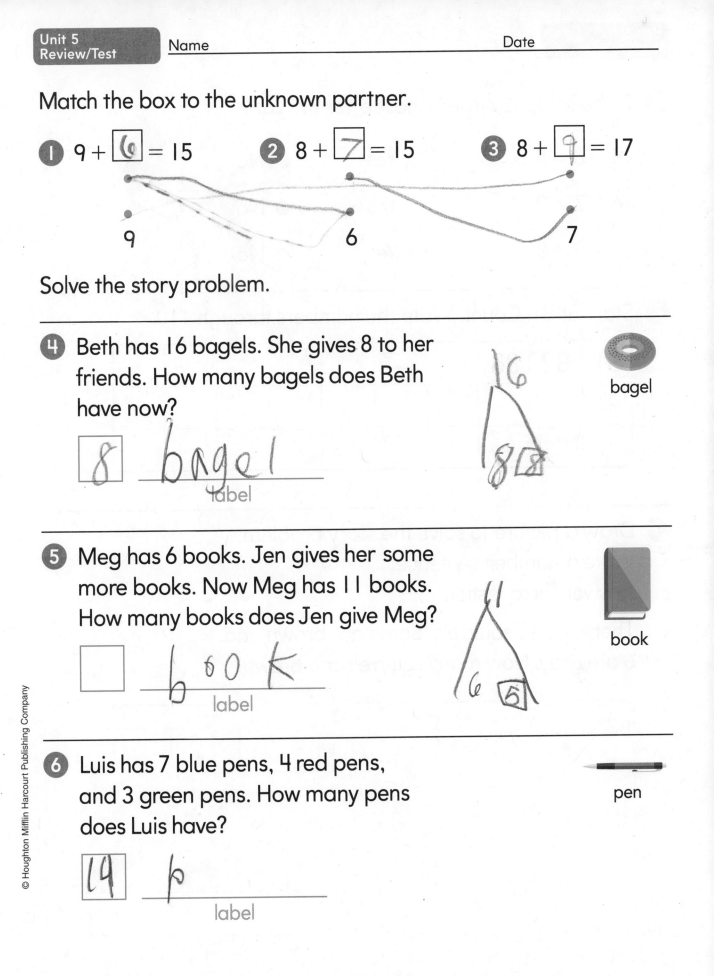

1 $9 + \boxed{6} = 15$ 2 $8 + \boxed{7} = 15$ 3 $8 + \boxed{9} = 17$

9   6   7

Solve the story problem.

4 Beth has 16 bagels. She gives 8 to her friends. How many bagels does Beth have now?

$\boxed{8}$ bagel
    label

bagel

5 Meg has 6 books. Jen gives her some more books. Now Meg has 11 books. How many books does Jen give Meg?

$\boxed{}$ book
    label

book

6 Luis has 7 blue pens, 4 red pens, and 3 green pens. How many pens does Luis have?

$\boxed{14}$ p
    label

pen

© Houghton Mifflin Harcourt Publishing Company

7 Is the sentence true? Choose Yes or No.

$14 - 8 = 5$	○ Yes	◉ No
$16 - 7 = 9$	◉ Yes	○ No
$17 - 9 = 8$	◉ Yes	○ No

8 Start at 81. Count. Write the numbers through 110.

81	82	83	84	85	86	87			
91									

9 Draw a picture to solve the story problem.
Write a number sentence.
Answer the question.

There are 15 squirrels. Some are brown and
6 are gray. How many squirrels are brown?

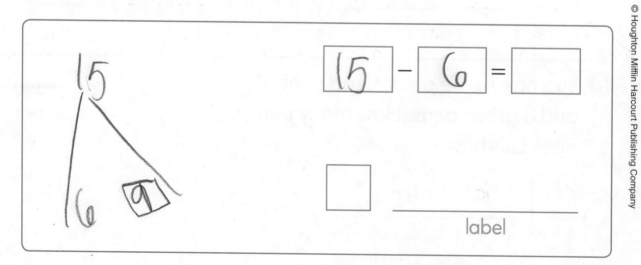

$$\boxed{15} - \boxed{6} = \boxed{}$$

label

Solve.

10 57 + 20 = 77

11 13 + 60 = 73 | | | | | | | 000

12 80 − 40 = 46

13 70 − 50 = 20

14 80 + 20 = 100

15 90 − 20 = 70

Ring the number that makes the sentence true.

16 There are 9 red crayons, 3 green crayons, and 7 blue crayons in the box. How many crayons are in the box?

crayon

> 10
> 16   crayons are in the box.
> (19)

---

17 There are 14 birds in a tree. Some birds fly away. Now there are 6 birds. How many birds fly away?

bird

> 6
> 8   birds fly away.
> 14

18 There are 12 boys and girls on the bus.
How many boys and girls can there be?
Choose all possible answers.

- ○ 2 boys and 14 girls
- ○ 2 boys and 10 girls
- ○ 3 boys and 9 girls
- ○ 4 boys and 6 girls
- ○ 5 boys and 7 girls

19 Draw 20 to 30 more triangles.
Ring 10-groups. Count by tens and ones.
Write the numbers.

△ △ △ △ △ △ △ △ △ △

△ △ △ △ △ △ △ △ △ △

△ △ △ △ △ △ △ △ △ △

△ △ △ △ △ △ △ △ △ △

△ △ △ △ △ △

The number of triangles is _____ .

10 less is _____ . 10 more is _____ .

Beach Day

Dan and Win look for shells at the beach.

1 **Part A**

Dan finds 32 shells. Draw to show 32 with tens and ones.

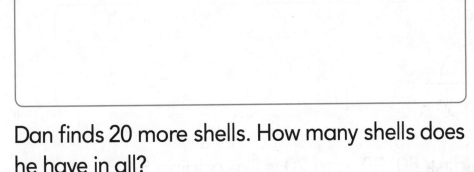

Dan finds 20 more shells. How many shells does he have in all?

☐ shells

Part B

Draw or tell how you know.

---

2 **Part A**

Win finds 5 white shells, 3 brown shells, and 2 black shells. How many shells does she have in all?

☐ shells

Part B

Draw or write to tell how you know.

Name _____

3 **Part A**

Win finds 50 white shells, 30 brown shells, and 20 black shells. How many shells does she have in all?

☐ shells

Part B

Draw or tell how you know.

☐

Part C

Tell how adding 50, 30, and 20 is like adding 5, 3, and 2.

☐

4 **Part A**

At noon, Win had 50 white shells.
At 4 P.M., Win had 80 white shells.
How many shells did she find after noon?

☐ shells

Part B

Draw or tell how you know.

☐

Dear Family:

Children begin this unit by learning to organize, represent, and interpret data with two and three categories.

In the example below, children sort apples and bananas and represent the data using circles. They ask and answer questions about the data and learn to express comparative statements completely.

There are 2 more bananas than apples.

There are 2 fewer apples than bananas.

Later in the unit, children solve *Compare* story problems using comparison bars. Two examples are given below.

Jeremy has 10 crayons.
Amanda has 3 crayons.
How many more crayons does Jeremy have than Amanda?

Abby has 8 erasers.
Ramon has 6 more erasers than Abby has. How many erasers does Ramon have?

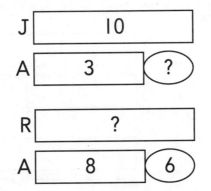

While working on homework, ask your child to explain to you how to use comparison bars to solve these types of story problems.
If you have any questions, please do not hesitate to contact me.

Sincerely,
Your child's teacher

CC SS Unit 6 addresses the following standards from the Common Core State Standards for Mathematics: **1.OA.A.1**, **1.OA.A.2**, **1.OA.C.6**, **1.OA.D.8**, **1.NBT.A.1**, **1.MD.C.4**, and all Mathematical Practices.

Estimada familia:

Al comenzar esta unidad, los niños aprenderán a organizar, representar e interpretar datos de dos y tres categorías.

En el ejemplo de abajo, los niños clasifican manzanas y plátanos, y representan los datos usando círculos. Formulan y responden preguntas acerca de los datos y aprenden cómo expresar enunciados comparativos completos.

Hay 2 plátanos más que manzanas.

Hay 2 manzanas menos que plátanos.

Más adelante en la unidad, los niños resolverán problemas que requieran *comparar*, usando barras de comparación. Abajo se dan dos ejemplos.

Jeremy tiene 10 crayones.
Amanda tiene 3 crayones.
¿Cuántos crayones más que
Amanda tiene Jeremy?

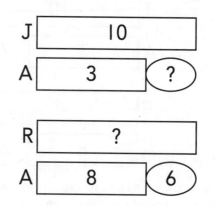

Abby tiene 8 borradores.
Ramón tiene 6 borradores
más que Abby. ¿Cuántos
borradores tiene Ramón?

Mientras hace la tarea, pida a su niño que le explique cómo usar las barras de comparación para resolver este tipo de problemas.

Si tiene alguna pregunta, no dude en comunicarse conmigo.

Atentamente,
El maestro de su niño

En la Unidad 6 se aplican los siguientes estándares de los Estándares estatales comunes de matemáticas: 1.OA.A.1, 1.OA.A.2, 1.OA.C.6, 1.OA.D.8, 1.NBT.A.1, 1.MD.C.4 y todos los de Prácticas matemáticas.

246 UNIT 6 LESSON 1   Explore Representing Data

data	more
fewer	most
fewest	sort

Eggs Laid This Month

Clucker

Vanilla

Vanilla laid **more** eggs than Clucker.

Colors in the Bag								
Red	◯	◯	◯					
Yellow	◯	◯	◯	◯	◯	◯	◯	
Blue	◯	◯	◯	◯	◯	◯		

The **data** show how many of each color.

Eggs Laid This Month

Clucker

Vanilla

Daisy

Vanilla laid the **most** eggs.

Eggs Laid This Month

Clucker

Vanilla

Clucker laid **fewer** eggs than Vanilla.

You can **sort** the animals into groups.

Eggs Laid This Month

Clucker

Vanilla

Daisy

Clucker laid the **fewest** eggs.

Name _____

1 Use circles and 5-groups to record.
Write how many in each group.

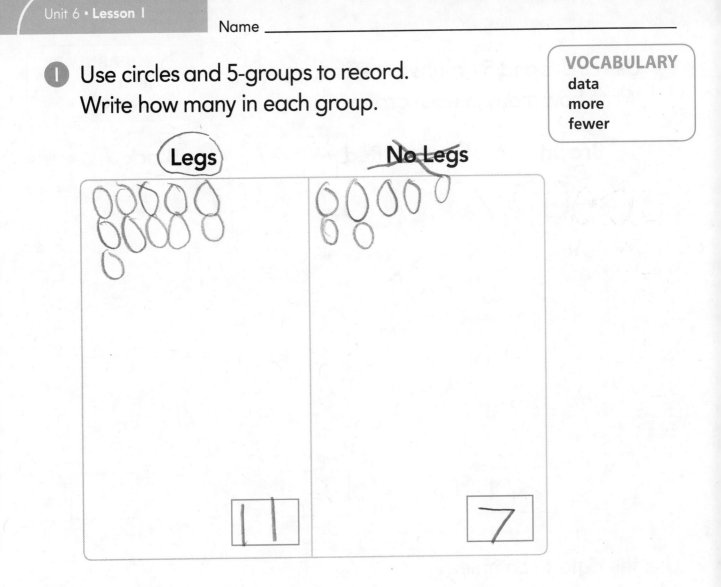

Legs   No Legs

11   7

Use the **data** to complete.

18

2 How many animals in all? _____

3 Ring the group with **more** animals.

4 Cross out the group with **fewer** animals.

5 Use circles and 5-groups to record.
Write how many in each group.

VOCABULARY
most
fewest

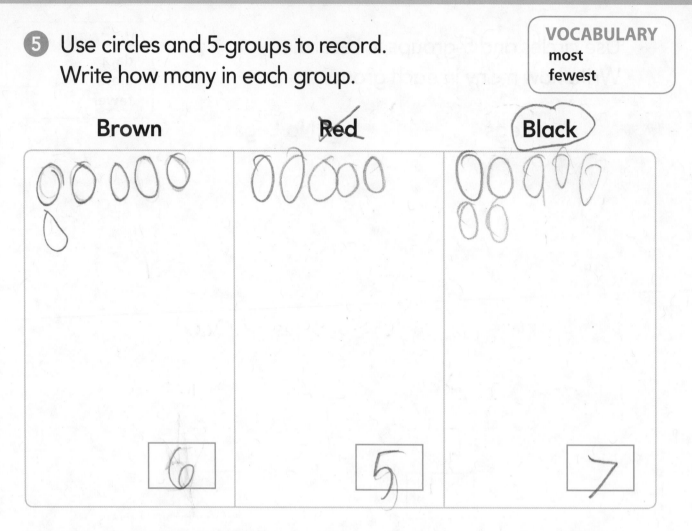

Brown   ~~**Red**~~   (**Black**)

| 6 | 5 | 7 |

Use the data to complete.

6 How many animals in all? **18**

7 Ring the group with the **most** animals.

8 Cross out the group with the **fewest** animals.

✓ **Check Understanding**

Draw circles and 5-groups to show
9 black animals and 8 green animals.

black animals:
green animals:

© Houghton Mifflin Harcourt Publishing Company

Explore Representing Data

1 Draw matching lines to compare.
Complete the sentences.
Ring the word **more** or **fewer**.

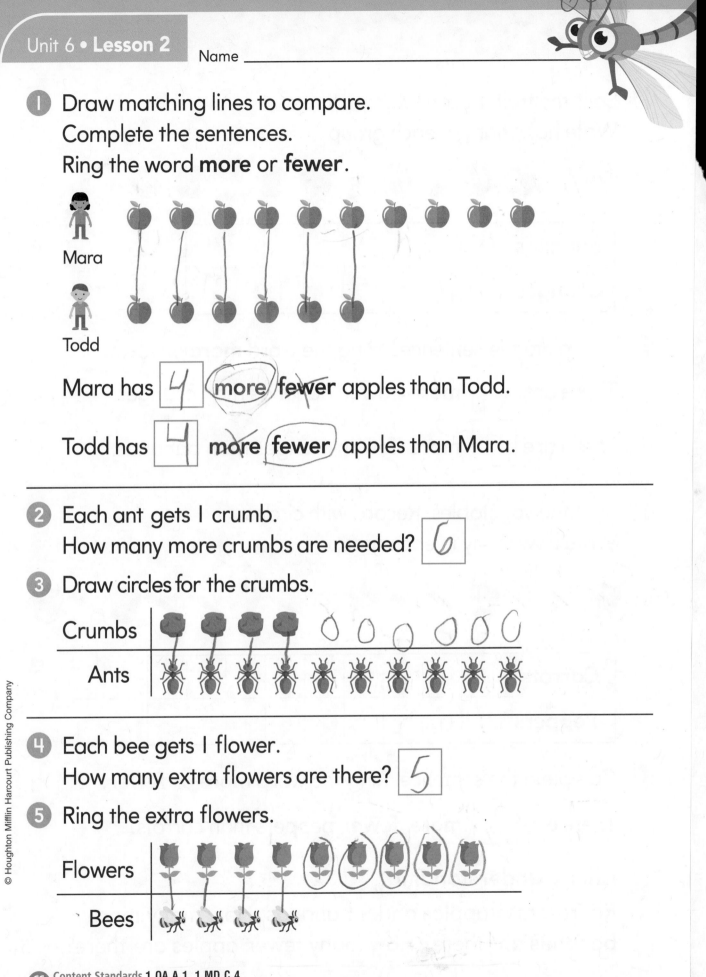

Mara

Todd

Mara has | 4 | (more) ~~fewer~~ apples than Todd.

Todd has | 4 | ~~more~~ (fewer) apples than Mara.

---

2 Each ant gets I crumb.
How many more crumbs are needed? | 6 |

3 Draw circles for the crumbs.

Crumbs

Ants

---

4 Each bee gets I flower.
How many extra flowers are there? | 5 |

5 Ring the extra flowers.

Flowers

Bees

© Houghton Mifflin Harcourt Publishing Company

6 Sort the fruit. Record with pictures.
Write how many in each group.

Bananas	0	0	0	0					4
Oranges	0	0	0	0	0	0	0	0	8

7 Complete the sentences. Ring the word **more** or **fewer**.

There are ☐4 ~~more~~ (**fewer**) bananas than oranges.

There are ☐4 (**more**) ~~fewer~~ oranges than bananas.

---

8 Sort the vegetables. Record with circles.
Write how many in each group.

Carrots	0	0	0	0	0	0	0	0	0	9
Peppers	0	0	0	0	0	0				6

9 Complete the sentence. Ring the word **more** or **fewer**.

There are ☐3 more (**fewer**) peppers than carrots.

✓ **Check Understanding**

Represent 5 apples and 9 bananas. How many more
bananas are there? How many fewer apples are there?

☐4 more ☐4 fewer

A 00000
B 000000 0000

Organize Categorical Data

1 Look at what Puzzled Penguin wrote.

Am I correct?

Stripes	O	O	O	O	O	O	O	O	O
Spots	O	O	O	O	O				

There are 4 more fish with stripes than with spots.

There are 4 fewer fish with spots than with stripes.

2 Help Puzzled Penguin.

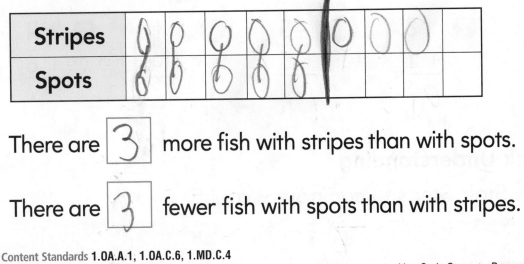

There are ⬚3⬚ more fish with stripes than with spots.

There are ⬚3⬚ fewer fish with spots than with stripes.

③ Sort the animals. Record with circles.
Write how many in each group.

| Dogs | 8 | 8 | 8 | 8 | 8 | 8 | 8 | | | 7 |
| Cats | 0 | 0 | 0 | 0 | 0 | 0 | 0 | 0 | 0 | 9 |

④ Complete the sentence. Ring the word **more** or **fewer**.

There are ⬚2 **more** (**fewer**) dogs than cats.

© Houghton Mifflin Harcourt Publishing Company

PATH to FLUENCY Add.

1. $\begin{array}{r} 4 \\ +3 \\ \hline 7 \end{array}$

2. $\begin{array}{r} 8 \\ +1 \\ \hline 9 \end{array}$

3. $\begin{array}{r} 5 \\ +5 \\ \hline 10 \end{array}$

4. $\begin{array}{r} 10 \\ +0 \\ \hline 10 \end{array}$

5. $\begin{array}{r} 4 \\ +6 \\ \hline 10 \end{array}$

✓ **Check Understanding**
Draw Stair Steps to compare 9 and 5.

Use Stair Steps to Represent Data

Name _____

1 Discuss the data.

2 Write how many in each category.

Eggs Laid This Month

$4 + 9 + 7 = 20$

20

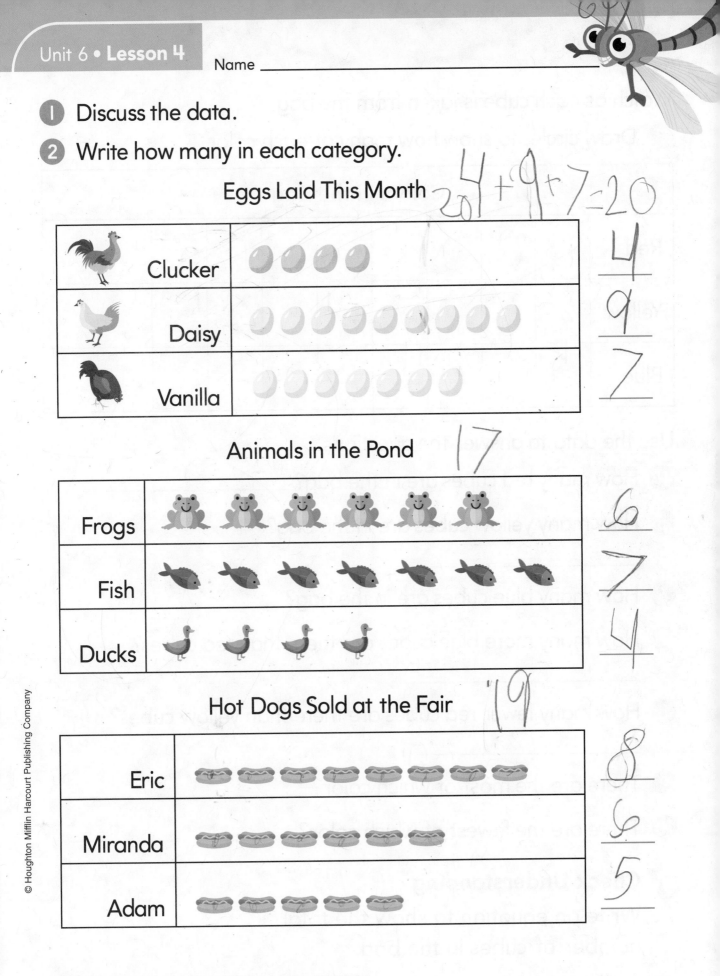

		Eggs		
	Clucker			4
	Daisy			9
	Vanilla			7

Animals in the Pond

17

Frogs		6
Fish		7
Ducks		4

Hot Dogs Sold at the Fair

19

Eric		8
Miranda		6
Adam		5

© Houghton Mifflin Harcourt Publishing Company

Watch as each cube is taken from the bag.

3 Draw circles to show how many of each color.

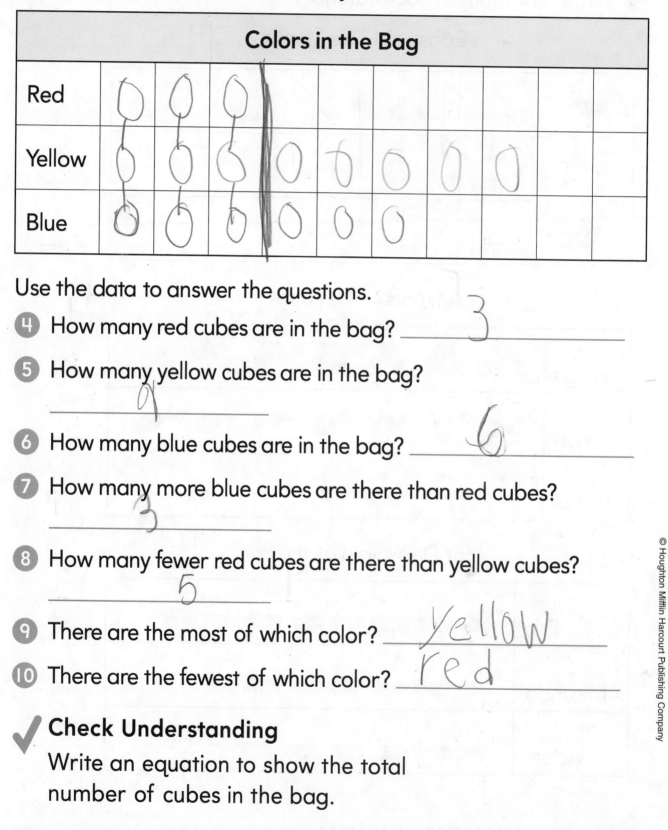

Colors in the Bag									
Red	O	O	O						
Yellow	O	O	O	O	O	O	O	O	
Blue	O	O	O	O	O	O			

Use the data to answer the questions.

4 How many red cubes are in the bag? ___3___

5 How many yellow cubes are in the bag?
___9___

6 How many blue cubes are in the bag? ___6___

7 How many more blue cubes are there than red cubes?
___3___

8 How many fewer red cubes are there than yellow cubes?
___5___

9 There are the most of which color? ___yellow___

10 There are the fewest of which color? ___red___

✓ Check Understanding

Write an equation to show the total
number of cubes in the bag.

Data Sets with Three Categories

Name _____

Use the data to answer the questions.

Favorite Vegetable

Corn	⊙ ⊙ ⊙ ⊙ ⊙ ⊙ ⊙
Carrots	⊙ ⊙ ⊙ ⊙ ⊙ ⊙ ⊙ ⊙ ⊙
Beans	⊙ ⊙ ⊙ ⊙

7
9
4

1 Which vegetable do the fewest people like?

2 How many more people like carrots than corn?

3 How many people voted altogether?

Beans

$9 - 7 = 2$ people

$7 + 9 + 4 = 20$ people

Favorite Animal

Parrot	⊙ ⊙ ⊙
Tiger	⊙ ⊙ ⊙ ⊙ ⊙ ⊙ ⊙ ⊙ ⊙ ⊙
Monkey	⊙ ⊙ ⊙ ⊙ ⊙ ⊙ ⊙

4 Which animal do the most people like?

_____

5 How many fewer people like monkeys than tigers?

_____

6 How many people like parrots best?

_____

Solve.

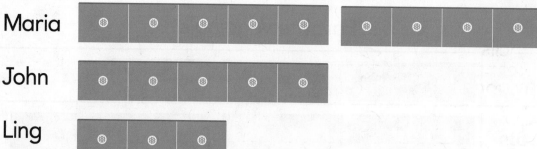

Maria

John

Ling

7 Maria has 9 dots. How many
fewer dots does Ling have
than Maria?

_____ dots

8 John has 5 dots. How many dots
does he need to take away to
have the same number as Ling?

_____ dots

9 John has 5 dots. How many dots
does John need to add to have as
many as Maria?

_____ dots

10 Teo has 5 more dots than Ling.
Draw to show Teo's dots.

✓ **Check Understanding**
Draw 3 Stair Steps of different lengths. Use
the terms more, fewer, most, and fewest to
compare the dots.

Data Collecting

Name

Date

1 Write how many in each group.

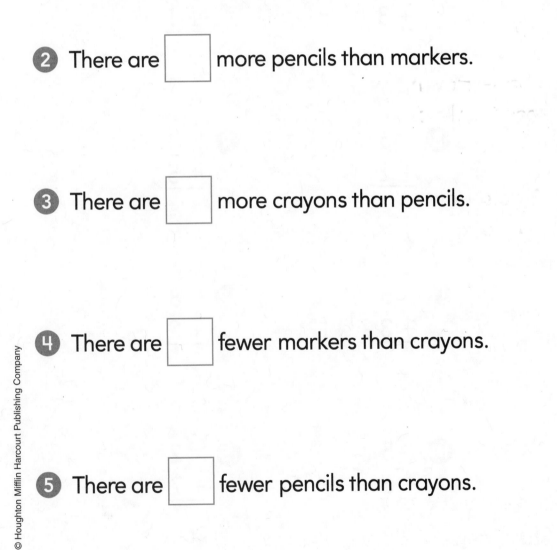

Pencils	◯	◯	◯	◯	◯	◯			
Crayons	◯	◯	◯	◯	◯	◯	◯	◯	
Markers	◯	◯							

Use the data to complete each sentence.

2 There are ☐ more pencils than markers.

3 There are ☐ more crayons than pencils.

4 There are ☐ fewer markers than crayons.

5 There are ☐ fewer pencils than crayons.

Name _____ Date _____

Add.

1. 1
    + 2

2. 3
    + 1

3. 2
    + 3

4. 2
    + 4

5. 4
    + 3

6. 6
    + 1

7. 4
    + 4

8. 5
    + 2

9. 4
    + 5

10. 6
    + 3

11. 5
    + 3

12. 8
    + 2

13. 6
    + 2

14. 5
    + 5

15. 2
    + 7

Name _____

Solve the story problem.
Use comparison bars.

Show your work.

1. Tessa has 15 pens.
Sam has 9 pens.
How many more pens
does Tessa have than Sam?

6 more pens
label

T | 15
S | 9 | 6

2. Tessa has 15 pens.
Sam has 9 pens.
How many fewer pens
does Sam have than Tessa?

6 fewer
label

T | 15
S | 9 | 6

3. Tessa has 15 pens. Sam has
6 fewer pens than Tessa. How
many pens does Sam have?

9 pens
label

T | 15
S | 9 | 6

4. Sam has 9 pens. Tessa has
6 more than Sam. How many
pens does Tessa have?

15 pens
label

T | 15
S | 9 | 6

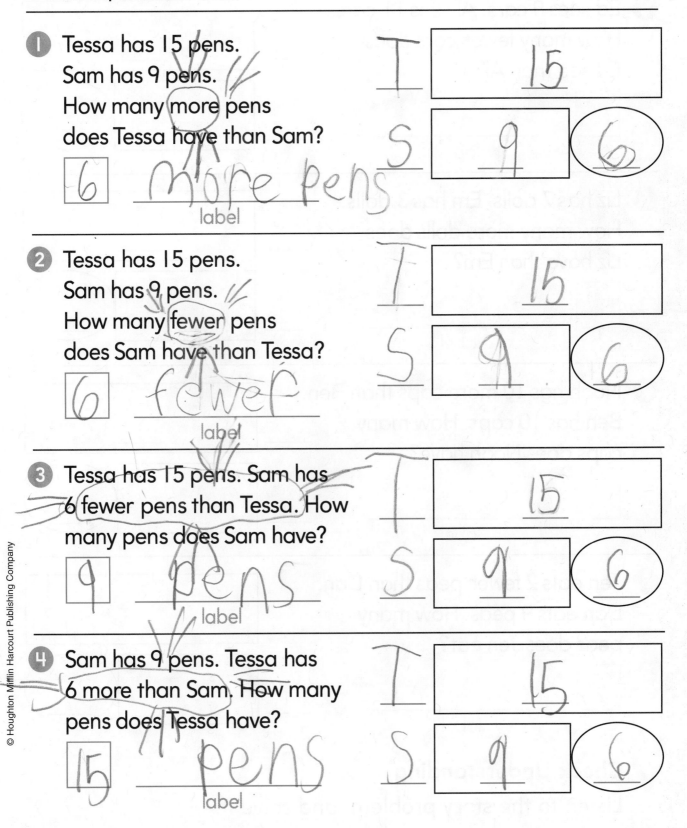

Solve the story problem. Use comparison bars.   **Show your work.**

5 Ed sees 9 cars. Al sees 11 cars. How many fewer cars does Ed see than Al?

☐ _____
　　　label

6 Liz has 7 dolls. Em has 3 dolls. How many more dolls does Liz have than Em?

☐ _____
　　　label

7 Noah has 10 more caps than Ben. Ben has 10 caps. How many caps does Noah have?

☐ _____
　　　label

8 Jen eats 2 fewer peas than Dan. Dan eats 9 peas. How many peas does Jen eat?

☐ _____
　　　label

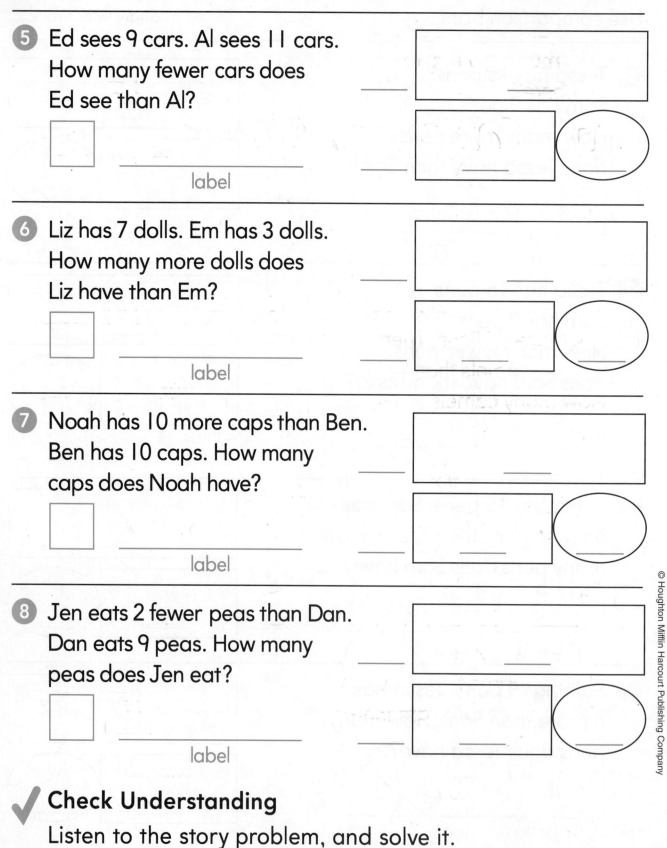

✓ **Check Understanding**

Listen to the story problem, and solve it.

Introduce Comparison Bars

Name _____

Solve and discuss.

1. There are 14 tigers and 8 bears.
How many more tigers than bears
are there?

| 6 | more tigers |
| label | |

$14 = 8 + 6$

$14 - 8 = 6$

T | 14
B | 8 | 6

14
／＼
8   6

2. There are 12 lions. There are
5 fewer camels than lions.
How many camels are there?

| 7 | |
| label | |

$5 + 7 = 12$

$12 - 5 = 7$

L | 12
C | | 5

12
／＼
7   5

3. There are 7 elephants. There are
6 more zebras than elephants.
How many zebras are there?

| 13 | zebras |
| label | |

$7 + 6 = 13$

Z | 13
E | 7 | 6

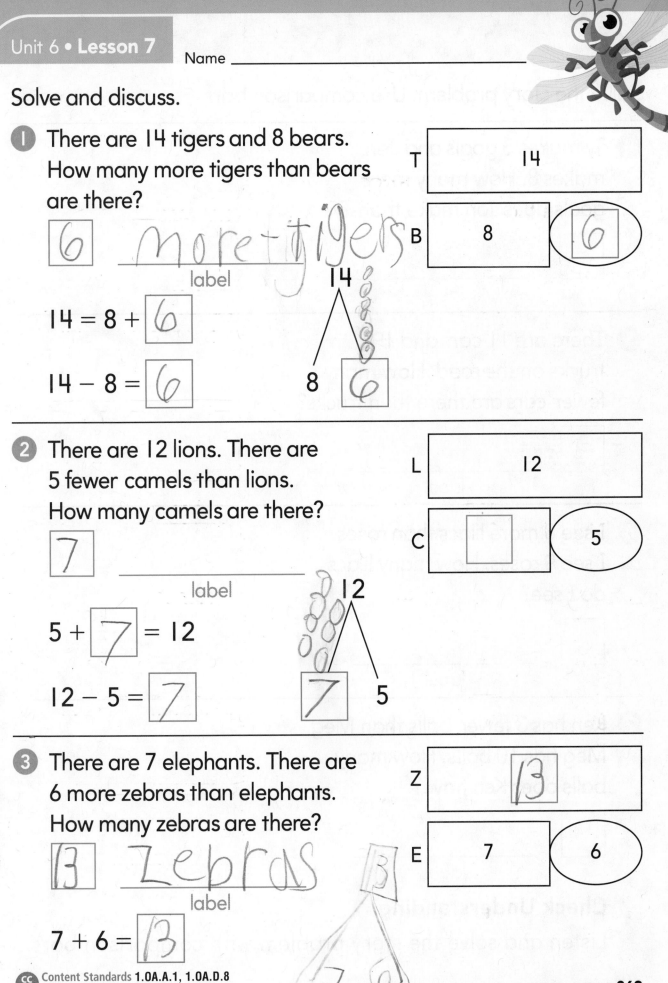

Solve the story problem. Use comparison bars.   **Show your work.**

4 Ty makes 5 goals and Jon makes 8. How many more goals does Jon make than Ty?

[3] ___more goals___
label

5 There are 11 cars and 19 trucks on the road. How many fewer cars are there than trucks?

[ ] _____
label

6 I see 8 more lilacs than roses. I see 9 roses. How many lilacs do I see?

[ ] _____
label

7 Ken has 3 fewer balls than Meg. Meg has 10 balls. How many balls does Ken have?

[ ] _____
label

✓ **Check Understanding**

Listen and solve the story problem with comparison bars.

Comparison Bars and Comparing Language

Solve the story problem.
Use comparison bars.

Show your work.

① Cory's cat has 11 kittens.
Eva's cat has 3 kittens.
How many fewer kittens does
Eva's cat have than Cory's?

☐ _____
label

② There were 3 bicycles here
yesterday. There are 7 more
bicycles here today. How many
bicycles are here today?

☐ _____
label

③ Ms. Perez has 15 horses.
Mr. Drew has 9 horses.
How many more horses does
Ms. Perez have than Mr. Drew?

☐ _____
label

Solve the story problem. Use comparison bars.   **Show your work.**

4 Jim pops 5 fewer balloons than Sadie. Jim pops 9 balloons. How many balloons does Sadie pop?

⬚ _____
                label

5 Nick hikes 12 miles in the forest. Nick hikes 4 more miles than Zia. How many miles does Zia hike?

⬚ _____
                label

PATH to FLUENCY Subtract.

1   9
       − 1

2   6
       − 3

3   8
       − 6

4   5
       − 5

5   9
       − 7

6   4
       − 2

7   10
       − 6

8   9
       − 3

9   7
       − 5

10   6
       − 1

✓ **Check Understanding**

Listen to the story problem, and use comparison bars and an equation to solve.

Solve Compare Problems

Name _____

Liam collects data at the park. He wants to know how many animals can fly and how many animals cannot fly.

1 Sort the animals.
Record with circles and 5-groups.

Animals That Can Fly	Animals That Cannot Fly

Use the data to complete.

2 How many animals can fly? _____

3 How many animals cannot fly? _____

4 How many animals does Liam see in all?

_____

5 How many more animals can fly than cannot fly?

_____

Solve.
Show your work.

6 There are 8 swings.
12 children want to swing.
How many children must
wait to swing?

☐ _____
       label

7 10 bikes are on the rack.
7 children start to ride. How
many bikes do not have a rider?

☐ _____
       label

Focus on Mathematical Practices

Solve the story problem.
Use comparison bars.

Show your work.

1 Keith scores 10 points. Eric
scores 7 points. How many
fewer points does Eric score
than Keith?

K

E

_____ label

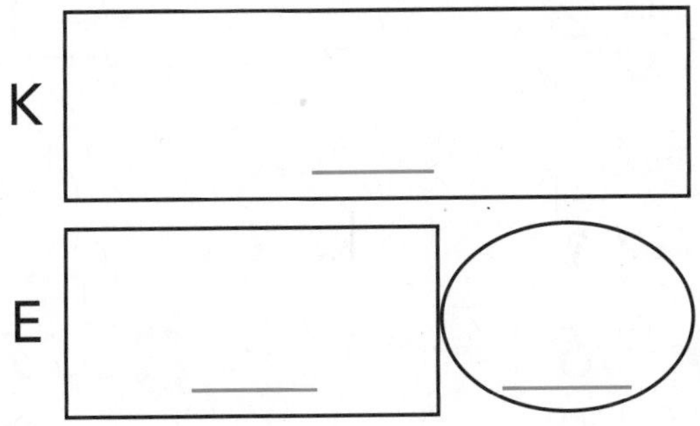

2 There are 2 more white rabbits
than brown rabbits. There are
9 brown rabbits. How many
white rabbits are there?

W

B

_____ label

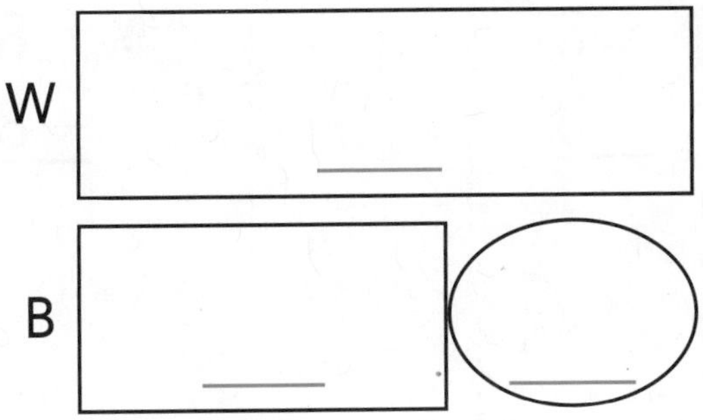

3 Don eats 6 more grapes than
Meg. Meg eats 12 grapes.
How many grapes does
Don eat?

D

M

_____ label

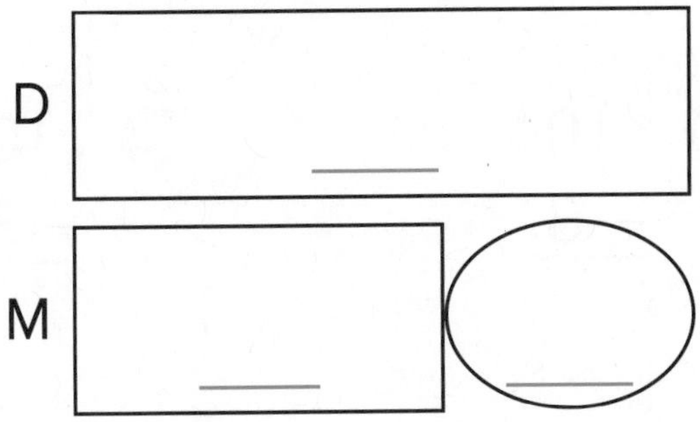

Name _____ Date _____

Subtract.

1
  4
− 2

2
  5
− 1

3
  3
− 3

4
  6
− 5

5
  7
− 4

6
  6
− 3

7
  8
− 3

8
  8
− 8

9
  7
− 2

10
  9
− 6

11
  8
− 5

12
  9
− 4

13
  10
− 3

14
  10
− 8

15
  9
− 3

1 Sort the animals. Record with circles.

2 Write how many in each group.

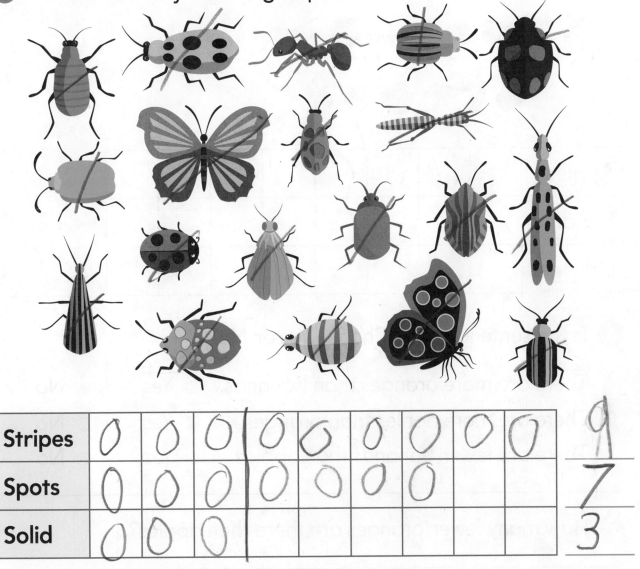

Stripes	O	O	O	O	O	O	O	O	O			9
Spots	O	O	O	O	O	O	O					7
Solid	O	O	O									3

Use the data. Choose the answer.

3 How many fewer <u>solid-color</u> animals
are there than animals with <u>stripes</u>?

○ 4   ● 6   ○ 7

4 How many animals are there in all?

○ 9   ○ 16   ● 19

5 Sort the fruit. Record with circles.
Write how many in each group.

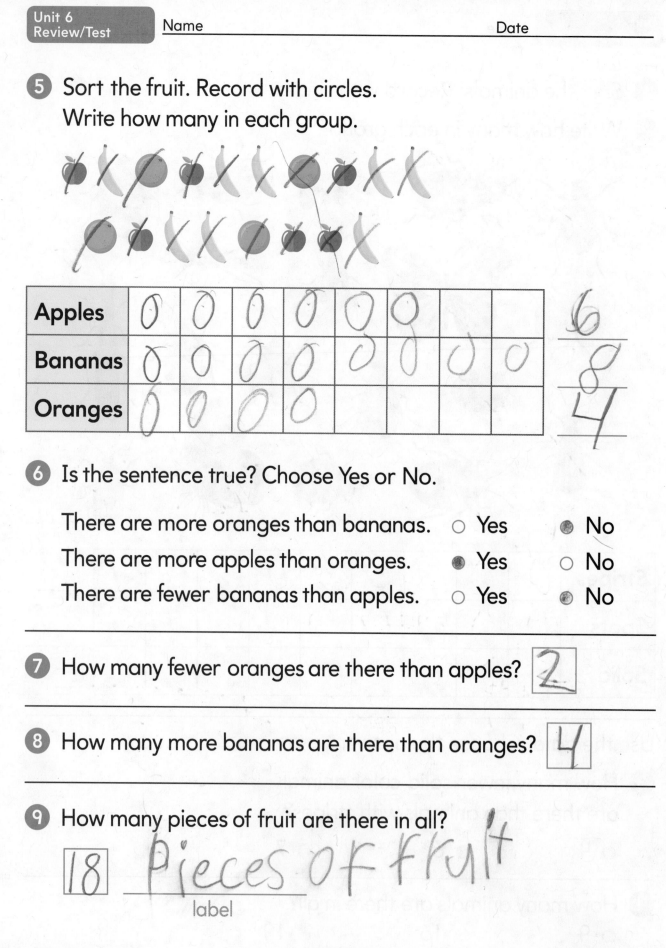

Apples	O	O	O	O	O	O			6
Bananas	O	O	O	O	O	O	O	O	8
Oranges	O	O	O	O					4

6 Is the sentence true? Choose Yes or No.

There are more oranges than bananas.   ○ Yes   ● No

There are more apples than oranges.   ● Yes   ○ No

There are fewer bananas than apples.   ○ Yes   ● No

---

7 How many fewer oranges are there than apples?   2

---

8 How many more bananas are there than oranges?   4

---

9 How many pieces of fruit are there in all?

18   Pieces of fruit
     _____label_____

Solve the story problem.
Use comparison bars.

10 Rico sees 5 more cats than dogs.
He sees 7 dogs.
How many cats does he see?

12	C A T S
	label

11 Nori has 15 coins.
Maria has 6 coins.
How many more coins does
Nori have than Maria?

9	more coins
	label

Ring the answer. Use comparison bars.

12 Kim picks 13 tulips.
Emily picks 8 tulips.
How many fewer tulips does
Emily pick than Kim?

Emily picks 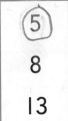 fewer tulips than Kim.

5
8
13

13 A class is going on a field trip. They collect data about places to go. Each child votes. The teacher draws one circle for each vote.

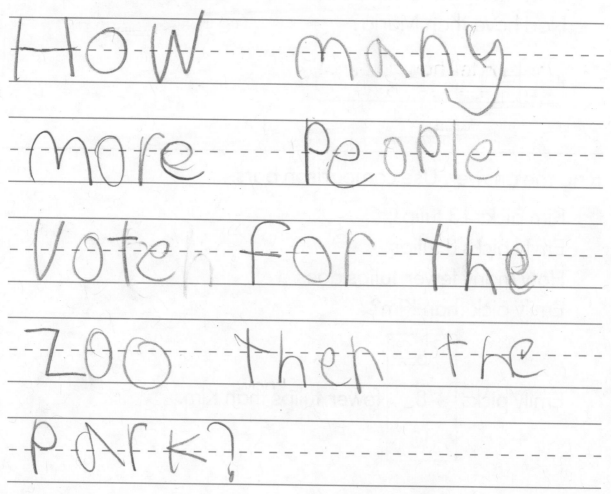

Field Trip Ideas

Park	Zoo	Museum
OOOOO	OOOOO OOOOO	OOOO

Write two questions about the data.
Answer each question.

How many
more people
voten for the
zoo then the
park?

Sort and Compare

Use all 20 strips of paper for this activity.

 Part A Sort the strips. Draw 5-groups and circles in the table to show how many strips you have of each color.

My Color Strips		
Red	**Blue**	**Yellow**

Part B How many strips are **not** blue?

☐ not blue

Draw or tell how you know.

2 **Part A** How many more strips are there of the color with the most strips than the color with the fewest strips? ☐

Part B Draw or tell how you know.

Compare Animals

Use the data to answer the questions.

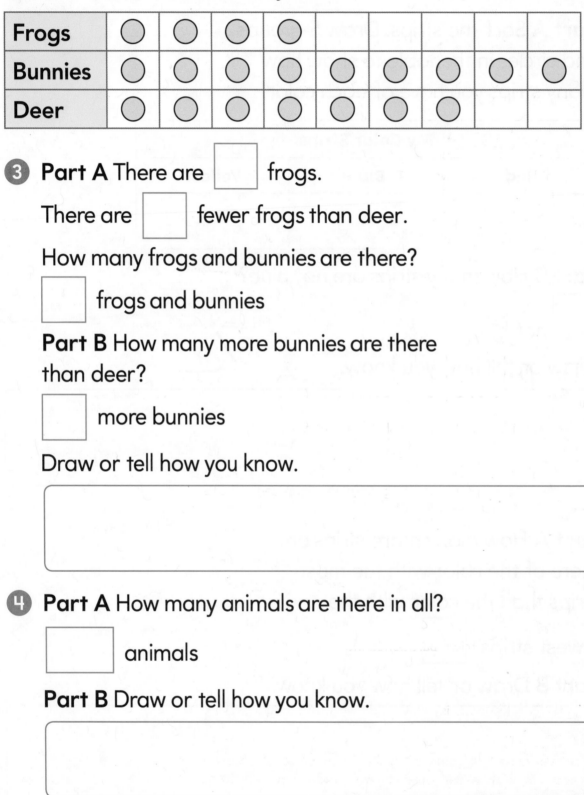

Frogs	○	○	○	○					
Bunnies	○	○	○	○	○	○	○	○	○
Deer	○	○	○	○	○	○	○		

3 **Part A** There are ⬜ frogs.

There are ⬜ fewer frogs than deer.

How many frogs and bunnies are there?

⬜ frogs and bunnies

Part B How many more bunnies are there than deer?

⬜ more bunnies

Draw or tell how you know.

⬜

4 **Part A** How many animals are there in all?

⬜ animals

Part B Draw or tell how you know.

⬜

Dear Family:

Your child has begun a unit that focuses on measurement and geometry. Children will begin the unit by learning to tell and write time in hours and half-hours on an analog and digital clock.

hour : minute

Later in the unit, children will work with both 2-dimensional and 3-dimensional shapes.

They will learn to distinguish between defining and non-defining attributes of shapes. For example, rectangles have four sides and four square corners. A square is a special kind of rectangle with all sides the same length. The shapes below are different sizes, colors, and orientations, but they are all rectangles.

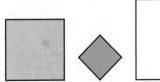

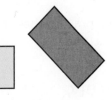

Later in the unit, children will compose shapes to create new shapes.

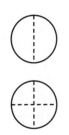

A cone and a rectangular prism were used to make this new shape.

Children will also learn to partition circles and rectangles into two and four equal shares. They describe the shares using the words *halves*, *fourths*, and *quarters*.

This circle is partitioned into halves.

This circle is partitioned into fourths or quarters.

Children generalize that partitioning a shape into more equal shares creates smaller shares: one fourth of the circle above is smaller than one half of the circle.

Another concept in this unit is length measurement. Children order three objects by length.

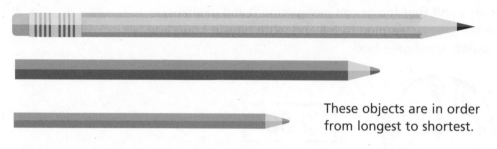

These objects are in order from longest to shortest.

They also use same-size length units such as paper clips to measure the length of an object.

This ribbon is 4 paper clips long.

You can help your child practice these new skills at home. If you have any questions, please contact me.

Sincerely,
Your child's teacher

© Houghton Mifflin Harcourt Publishing Company

CC SS **Unit 7 addresses the following standards from the** Common Core State Standards for Mathematics: **1.OA.C.6**, **1.MD.A.1**, **1.MD.A.2**, **1.MD.B.3**, **1.G.A.1**, **1.G.A.2**, **1.G.A.3**, and all Mathematical Practices.

Estimada familia:

Su niño ha comenzado una unidad sobre medidas y geometría. Comenzará esta unidad aprendiendo a leer y escribir la hora en punto y la media hora en un reloj analógico y en uno digital.

hora : minuto

Después, trabajará con figuras bidimensionales y tridimensionales.

Aprenderá a distinguir entre atributos que definen a una figura y los que no la definen. Por ejemplo, los rectángulos tienen cuatro lados y cuatro esquinas. Un cuadrado es un tipo especial de rectángulo que tiene lados de igual longitud. Las figuras de abajo tienen diferente tamaño, color y orientación, pero todas son rectángulos.

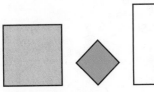

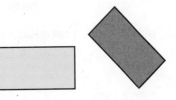

Más adelante en la unidad, los niños acomodarán figuras de diferentes maneras para formar nuevas figuras.

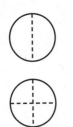
Para formar esta nueva figura se usaron un cono y un prisma rectangular.

También aprenderán a dividir círculos y rectángulos en dos y cuatro partes iguales. Describirán esas partes usando *mitades* y *cuartos*.

Este círculo está dividido en mitades.

Este círculo está dividido en cuartos.

Deducirán que si dividen un figura en más partes iguales, obtendrán partes más pequeñas: un cuarto del círculo es más pequeño que una mitad.

Otro concepto que se enseña en esta unidad es la medición de longitudes. Los niños ordenan tres objetos según su longitud.

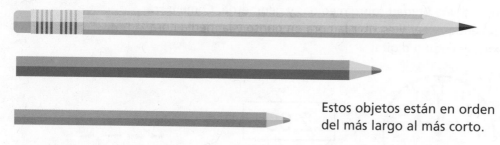

Estos objetos están en orden del más largo al más corto.

También usan unidades de la misma longitud, tales como clips, para medir la longitud de un objeto.

Esta cinta mide 4 clips de longitud.

Usted puede ayudar a su niño a practicar estas nuevas destrezas en casa. Si tiene alguna pregunta, comuníquese conmigo.

Atentamente,
El maestro de su niño

CC SS **En la Unidad 7 se aplican los siguientes estándares de los** Estándares estatales comunes de matemáticas: **1.OA.C.6, 1.MD.A.1, 1.MD.A.2, 1.MD.B.3, 1.G.A.1, 1.G.A.2, 1.G.A.3 y todos los de** Prácticas matemáticas.

Introduction to Time

circle

cube

clock

cylinder

cone

equal shares

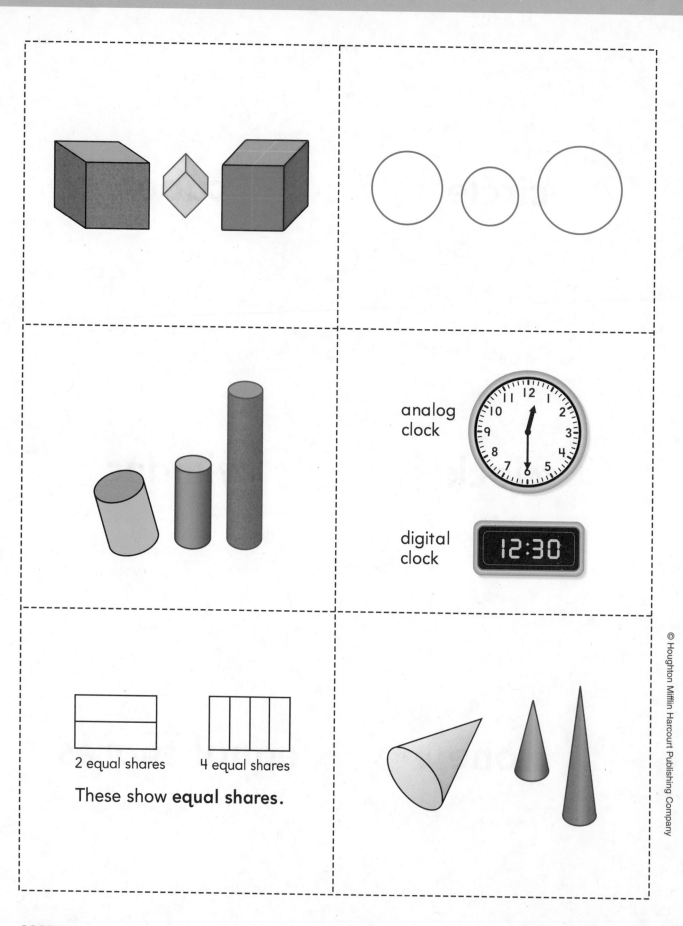

analog
clock

digital
clock

12:30

2 equal shares   4 equal shares

These show **equal shares.**

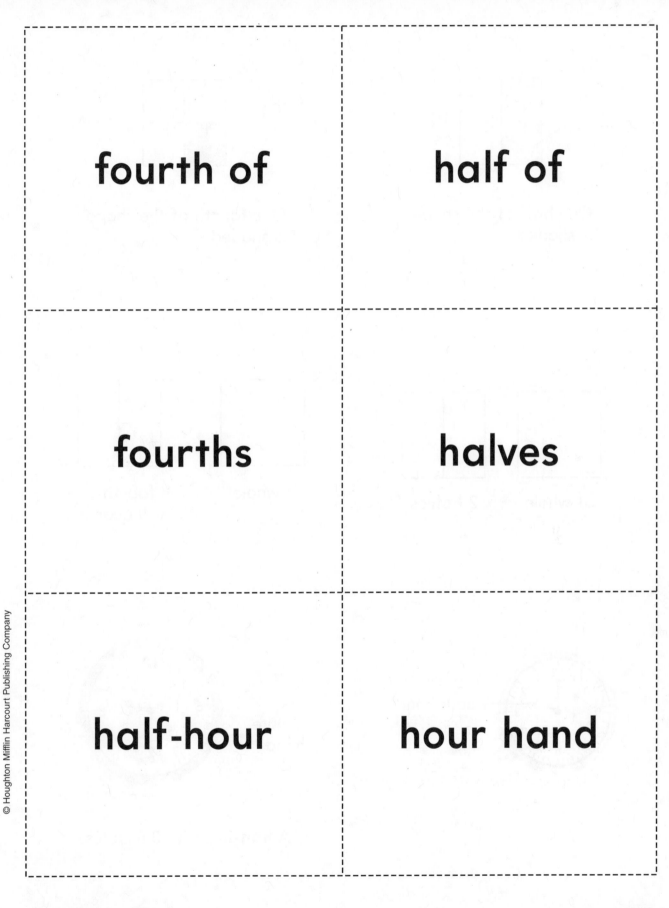

fourth of

half of

fourths

halves

half-hour

hour hand

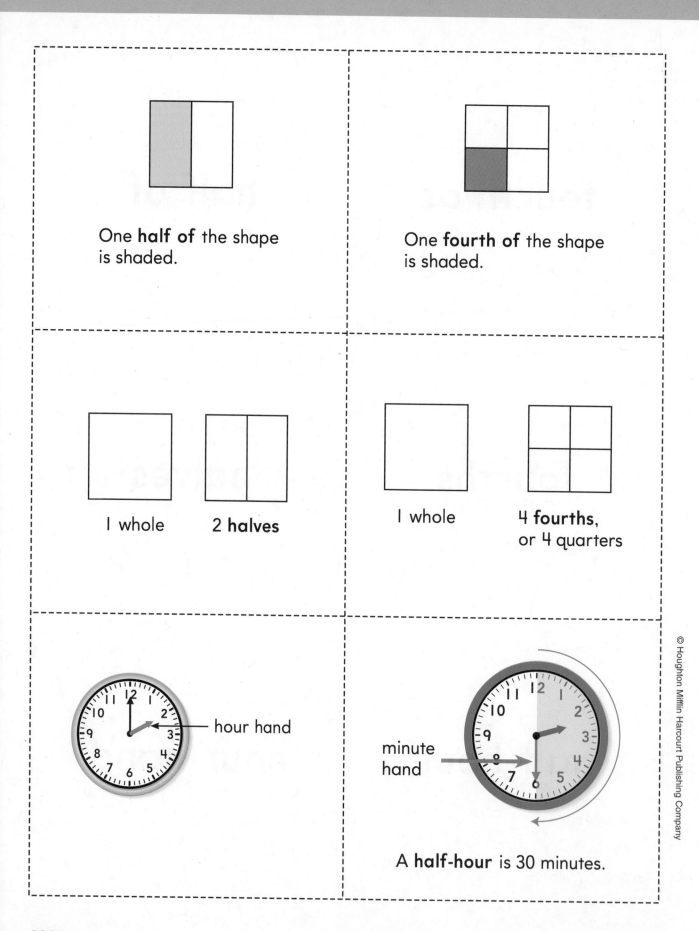

One **half of** the shape is shaded.

One **fourth of** the shape is shaded.

1 whole   2 **halves**

1 whole   4 **fourths**, or 4 quarters

hour hand

minute hand

A **half-hour** is 30 minutes.

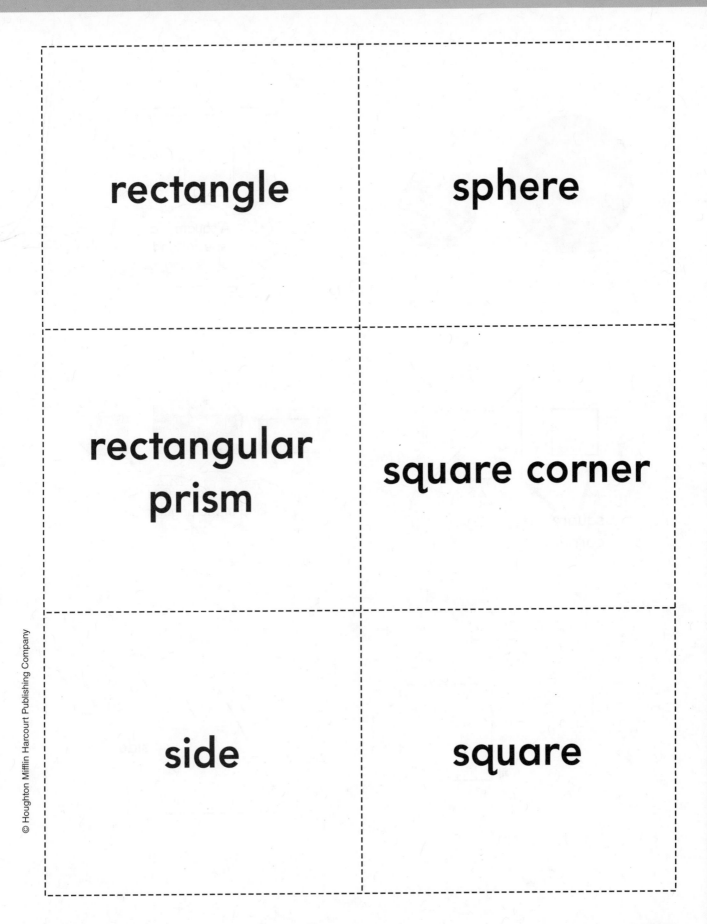

rectangle

sphere

rectangular prism

square corner

side

square

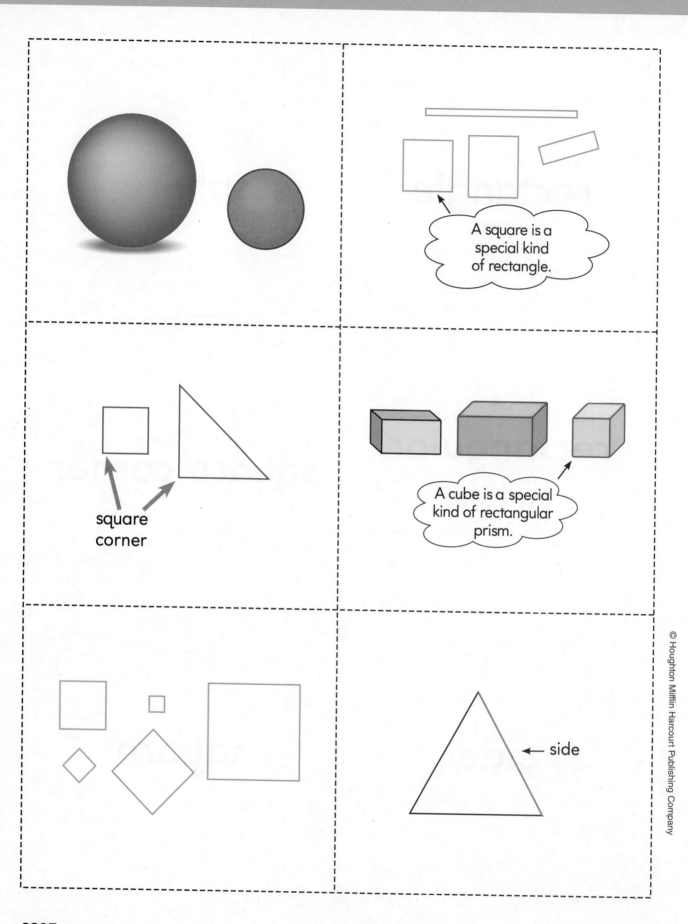

A square is a special kind of rectangle.

square corner

A cube is a special kind of rectangular prism.

side

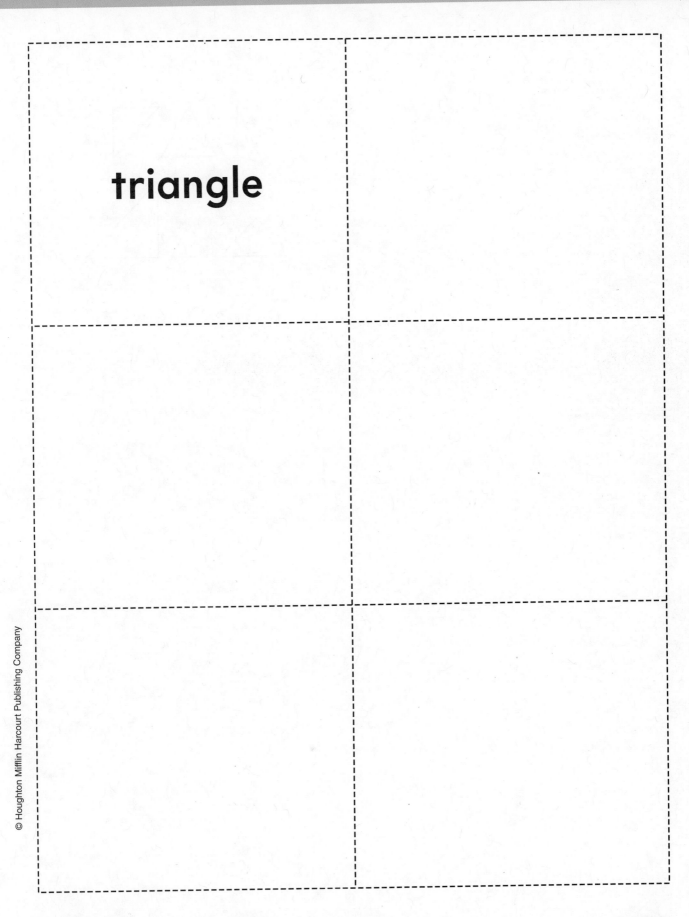

triangle

Write the number to show the time.

1   _____ o'clock

2   _____ o'clock

3   _____ o'clock

4   _____ o'clock

5   _____ o'clock

6   _____ o'clock

CC SS Content Standards **1.MD.B.3**
Mathematical Practices **MP5, MP6**

Draw lines to match the time.

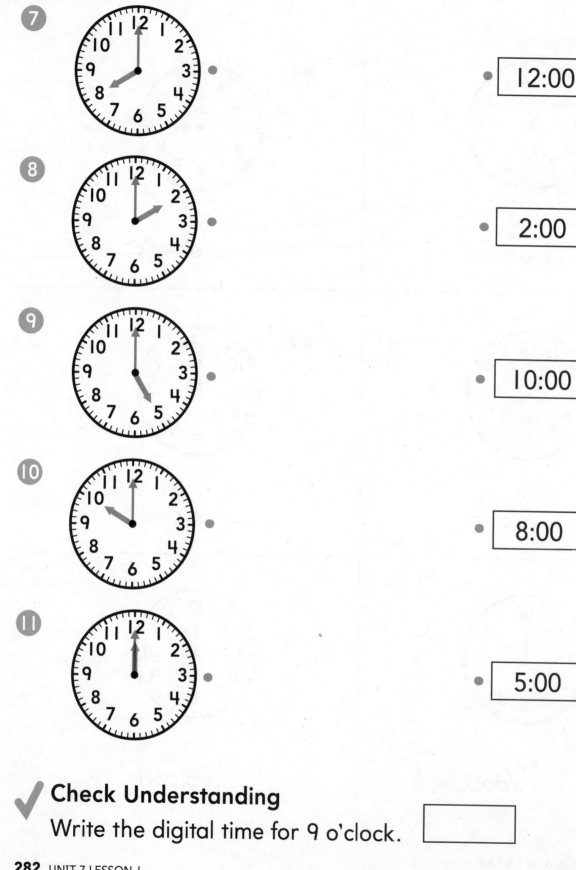

7   12:00

8   2:00

9   10:00

10   8:00

11   5:00

✓ Check Understanding

Write the digital time for 9 o'clock.

Introduction to Time

Name _____

VOCABULARY
clock

Read the **clock**.

Write the time on the digital clock.

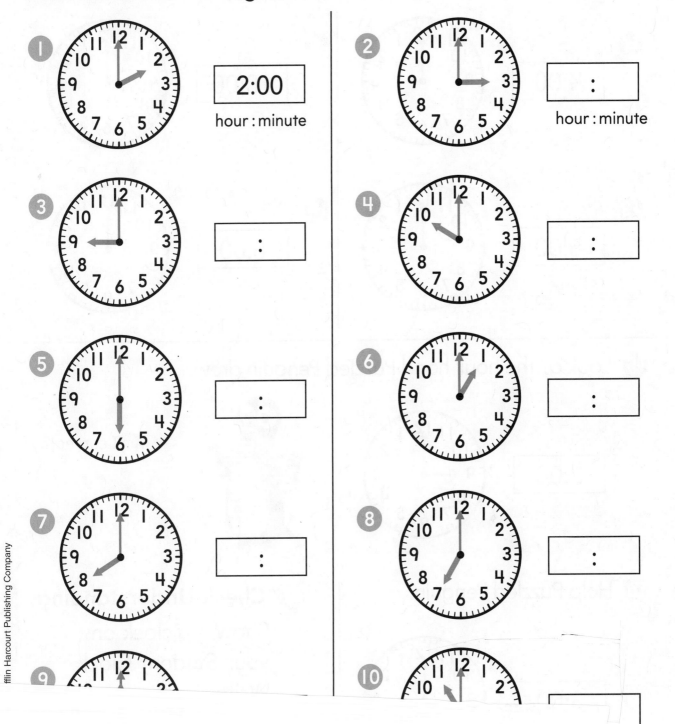

1. 2:00

hour : minute

2. :

hour : minute

3. :

4. :

5. :

6. :

7. :

8. :

9.

10.

Draw the **hour hand** on the clock
to show the time.

⓫ 4:00

⓬ 10:00

⓭ 5:00

⓮ 8:00

⓯ Look at the hour hand Puzzled Penguin drew.

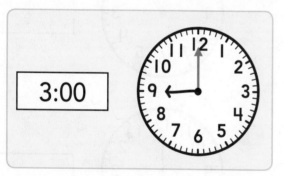

3:00

Am I correct?

⓰ Help Puzzled Penguin.

3:00

✔ **Check Understanding**

Show 7 o'clock on
your Student Clock.
Write the digital
time below.

Tell and Write Time in Hours

Clocks for "Our Busy Day" Book

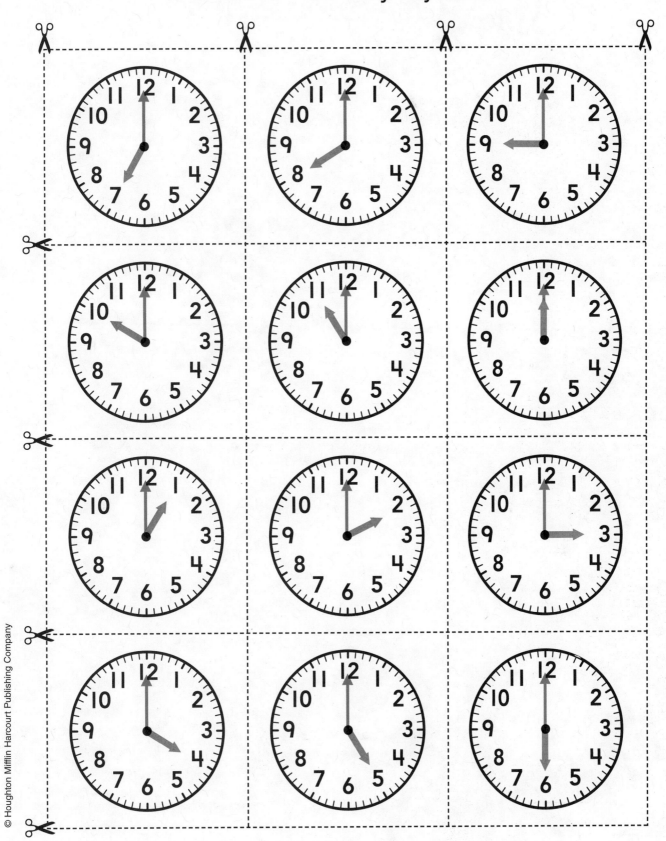

Clocks for "Our Busy Day" Book

Name _____

Read the clock.
Write the time on the digital clock.

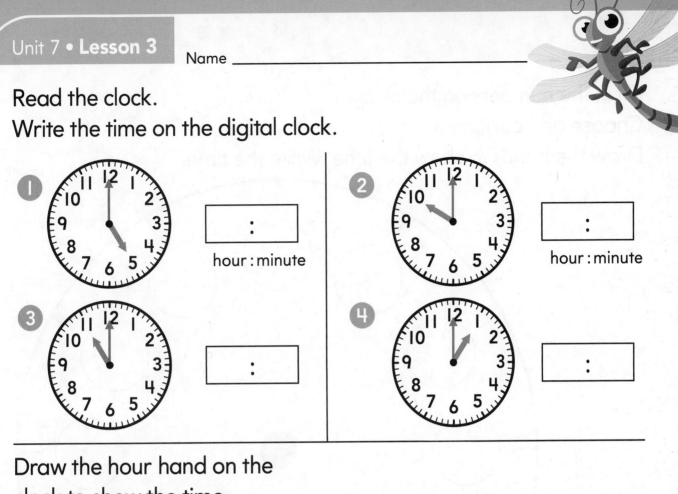

1. :
    hour : minute

2. :
    hour : minute

3. :

4. :

Draw the hour hand on the
clock to show the time.

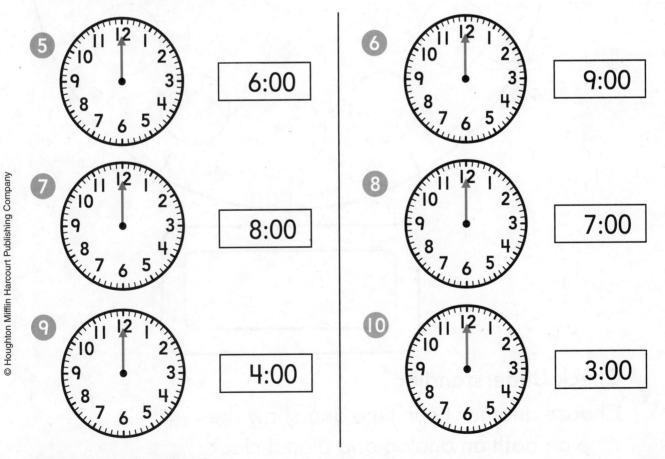

5. 6:00

6. 9:00

7. 8:00

8. 7:00

9. 4:00

10. 3:00

© Houghton Mifflin Harcourt Publishing Company

Fill in the numbers on the clock.

Choose an hour time.

Draw the hands to show the time. Write the time.

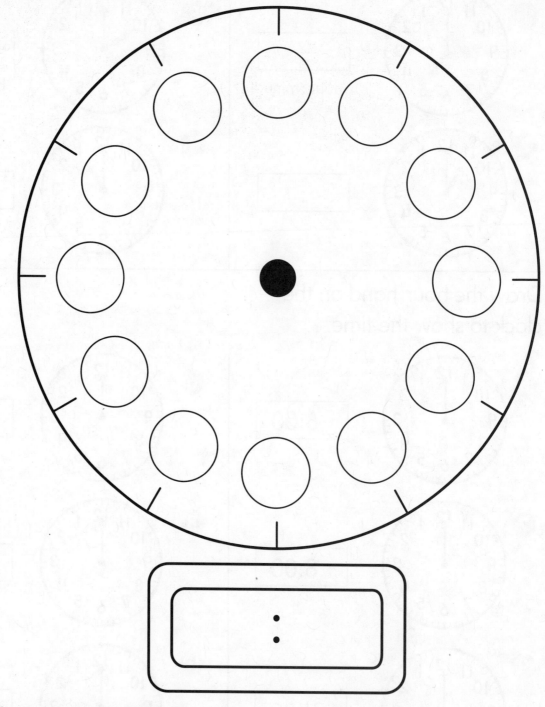

✔ Check Understanding

Choose another hour time and show the
time on both an analog and digital clock.

Name _____

VOCABULARY
half-hour

Read the clock.
Write the **half-hour** time on the digital clock.

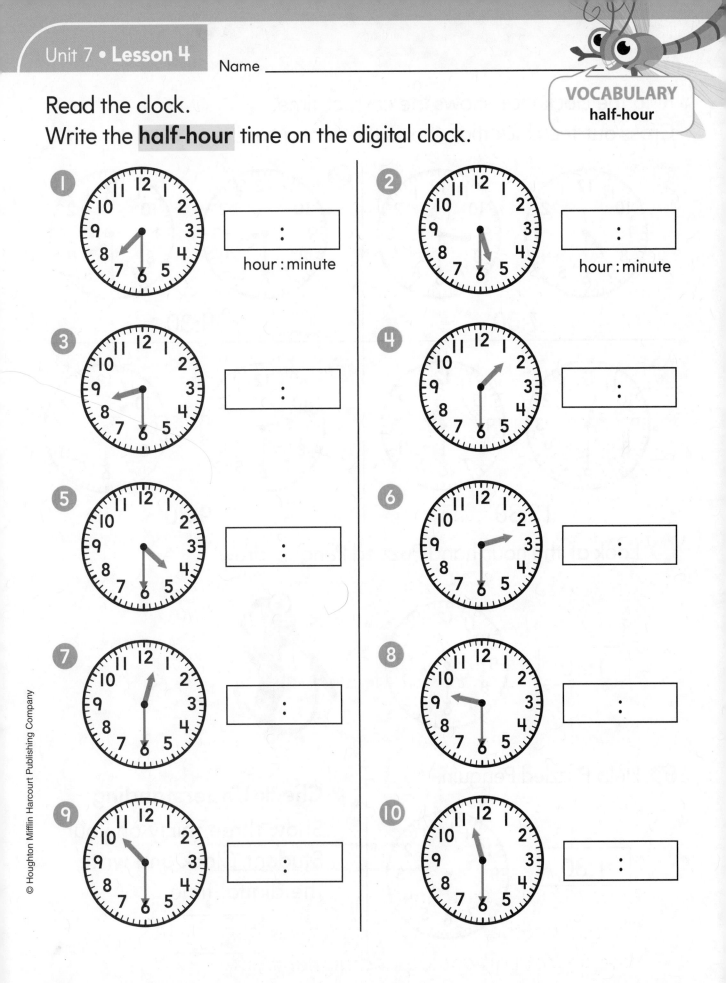

① ___ : ___   hour : minute

② ___ : ___   hour : minute

③ ___ : ___

④ ___ : ___

⑤ ___ : ___

⑥ ___ : ___

⑦ ___ : ___

⑧ ___ : ___

⑨ ___ : ___

⑩ ___ : ___

Ring the clock that shows the correct time.
Cross out the clock that shows the wrong time.

11   7:30

12   4:30

13   12:30

14   9:30

15 Look at the hour hand Puzzled Penguin drew.

1:30

Am I correct?

16 Help Puzzled Penguin.

1:30

✓ **Check Understanding**

Show three thirty on your Student Clock and write the digital time.

Name _____

Show the same half-hour time on both clocks.

Show the same time on both clocks.
Pick hour and half-hour times.

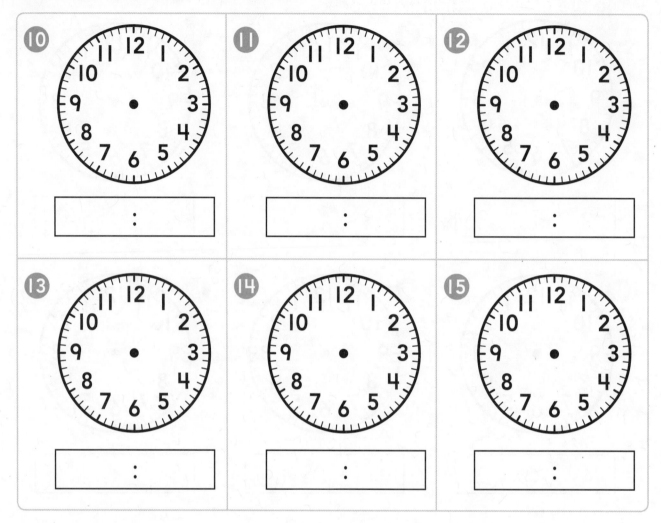

10 [:]

11 [:]

12 [:]

13 [:]

14 [:]

15 [:]

PATH to FLUENCY Find the unknown partner.

1 $4 + \boxed{} = 8$

2 $4 + \boxed{} = 10$

3 $8 + \boxed{} = 9$

✓ **Check Understanding**

Show eight thirty and eight o'clock on
your Student Clock and write the times.

[ ]   [ ]

Practice Telling and Writing Time

Name _____

Date _____

Read the clock.

Write the time on the digital clock.

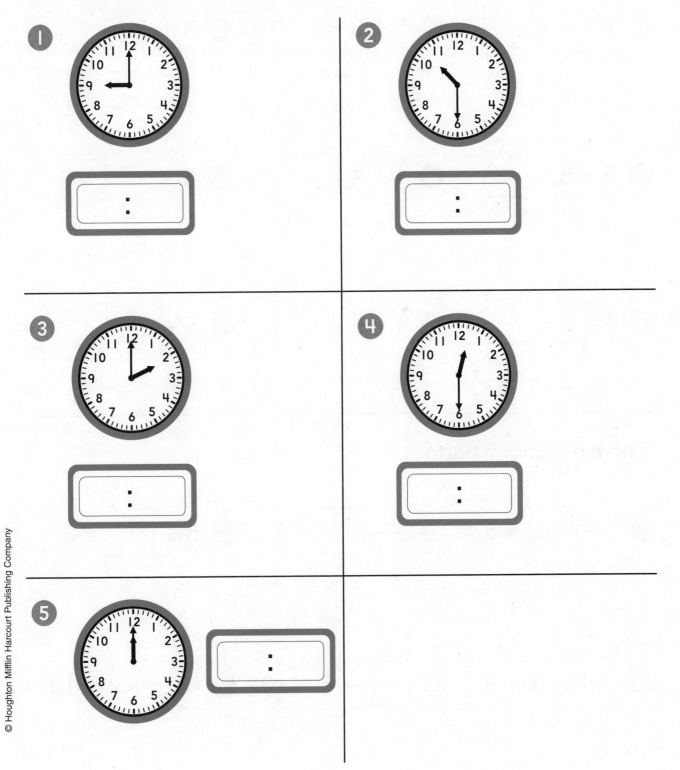

Name _____ Date _____

Add.

1 1 + 1 = ☐   2 5 + 3 = ☐   3 3 + 1 = ☐

4 5 + 5 = ☐   5 4 + 4 = ☐   6 5 + 1 = ☐

7 4 + 3 = ☐   8 4 + 5 = ☐   9 5 + 2 = ☐

Find the unknown partner.

10 1 + ☐ = 8   11 3 + ☐ = 6   12 5 + ☐ = 8

13 ☐ + 3 = 9   14 ☐ + 5 = 10   15 ☐ + 2 = 10

2-Dimensional Shape Set **297**

2-Dimensional Shape Set

2-Dimensional Shape Set **299**

2-Dimensional Shape Set

Name _____

1 Which shapes are NOT **rectangles** or **squares**? Draw an X on each one.

Draw the shape.

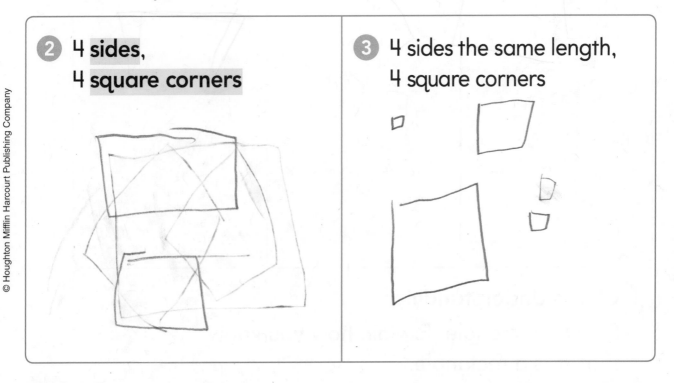

2 4 **sides,** 4 **square corners**

3 4 sides the same length, 4 square corners

4 Sort the shapes into three groups:
  • Squares
  • Rectangles That Are Not Squares
  • Not Squares or Rectangles

Draw each shape in the correct place on the sorting mat.

✓ **Check Understanding**

Draw a rectangle. Explain how you know that it is a rectangle.

Squares and Other Rectangles

Name _____

VOCABULARY
triangle
circle

1 Which shapes are NOT **triangles** or **circles**?
Draw an X on each one.

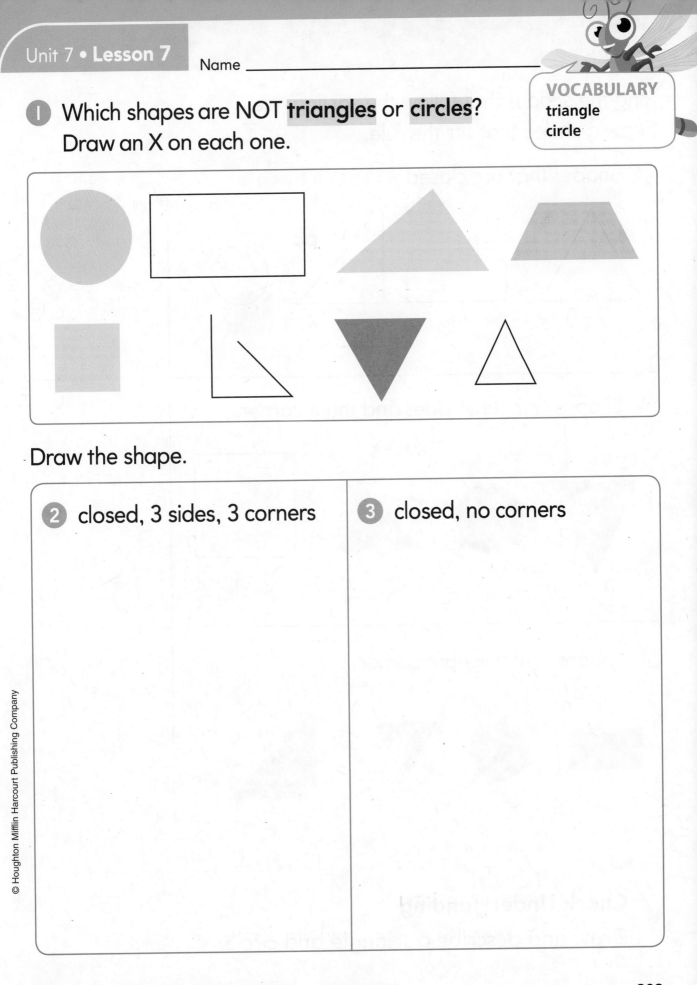

Draw the shape.

2 closed, 3 sides, 3 corners

3 closed, no corners

Ring the shapes that follow the sorting rule.
Draw a shape that fits the rule.

4 Shapes that are closed

5 Shapes with three sides and three corners

6 Shapes with a square corner

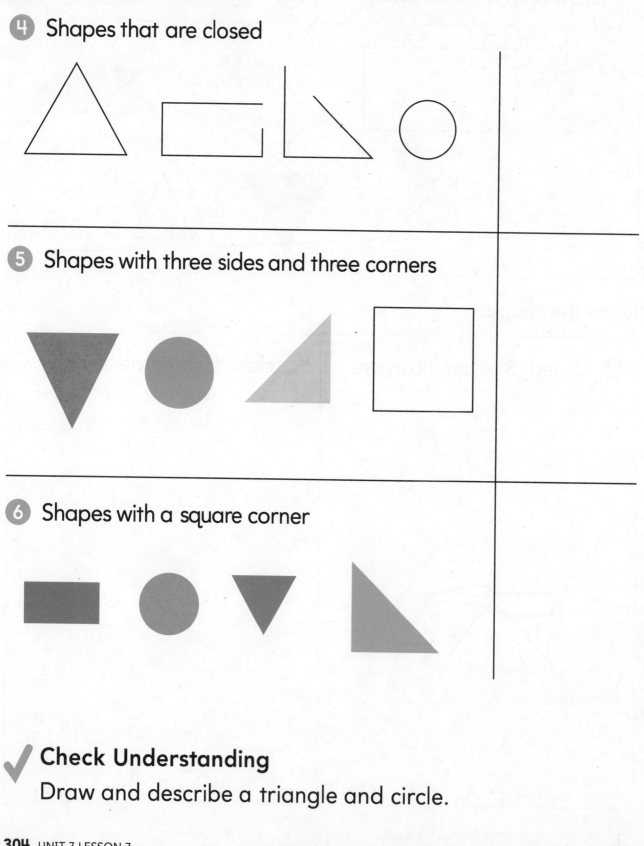

✓ **Check Understanding**
Draw and describe a triangle and circle.

Triangles and Circles

Name _____

VOCABULARY
halves

Cut out the shapes below.
How many ways can you fold them into **halves**?

Equal Shares

Name _____

Draw a line to show halves.
Color one **half of** the shape.

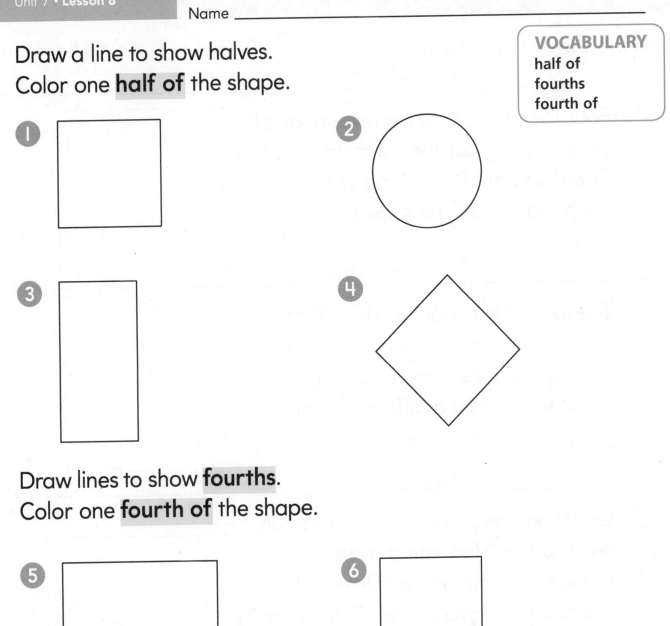

1

2

3

4

Draw lines to show **fourths**.
Color one **fourth of** the shape.

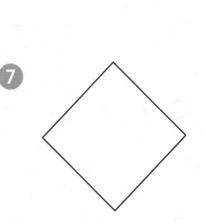

5

6

7

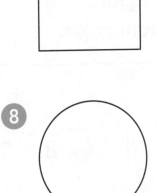

8

Solve the story problem.

9 Four friends want to share a sandwich.
How can they cut the sandwich into four
equal shares? Draw lines. Color
each share a different color.

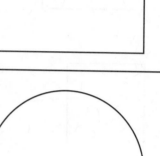

10 The four friends want to share a pie
for dessert. How can they cut the pie
into four equal shares? Draw lines.
Color each share a different color.

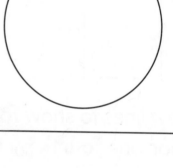

11 One friend only wants one half of her
granola bar. How can she cut her
granola bar into halves? Draw a line
to show two equal shares. Color each
share a different color.

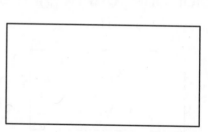

PATH to FLUENCY Subtract.

1 $10 - 3 = \boxed{}$ **2** $8 - 8 = \boxed{}$ **3** $9 - 1 = \boxed{}$

✓ **Check Understanding**
Show two equal shares of a circle.
Show four equal shares of a circle.

Equal Shares

Name _____

Build and draw the shape.

 Build a square. Use rectangles.

 Build a rectangle with all sides the same length.
Use triangles with a square corner.

---

3 Build a rectangle with two short sides and two
long sides. Use triangles and rectangles.

Compose 2-Dimensional Shapes

Name _____

Use 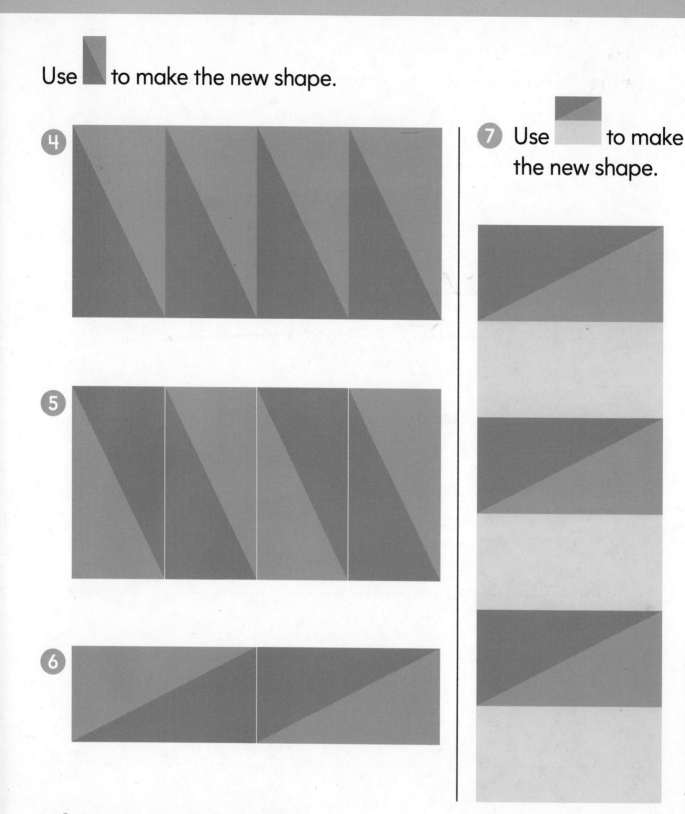 to make the new shape.

4

5

6

7 Use to make the new shape.

✓ Check Understanding

Explain how to use shapes to make
a new rectangle and triangle.

Compose 2-Dimensional Shapes

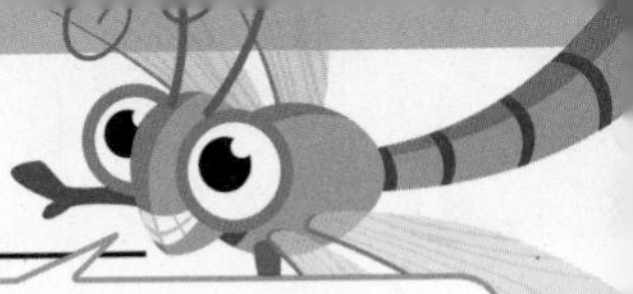

Shape Names
cone
cube
cylinder
rectangular prism
sphere

Draw a line to match like shapes.
Write the name of the shape.

1 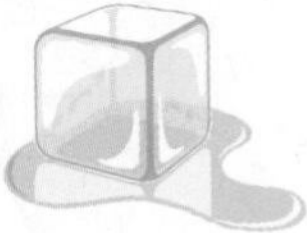 sphere

2 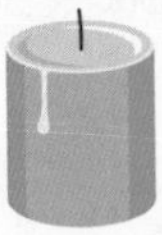 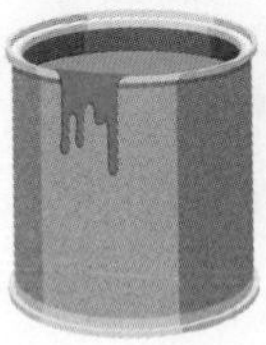 cylinder

3 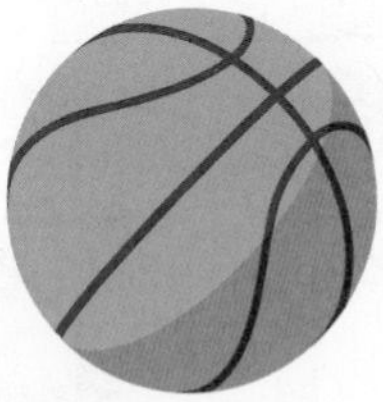 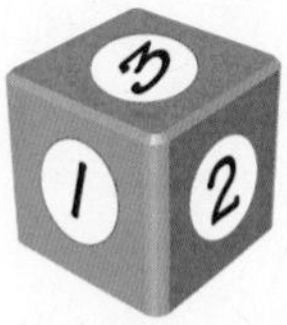 Cube

4 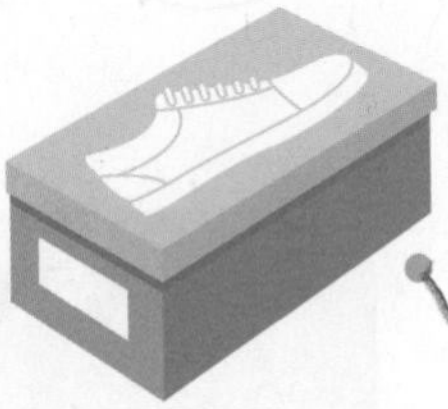 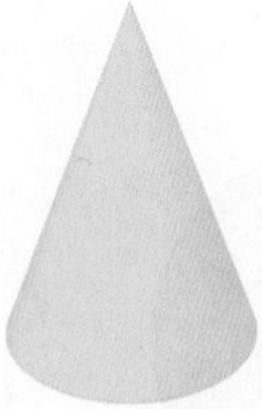 cone

5 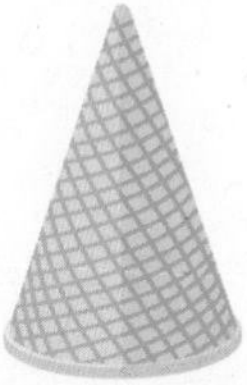 rectangular prism

6 Which shapes are NOT **rectangular prisms?**
Draw an X on each one.

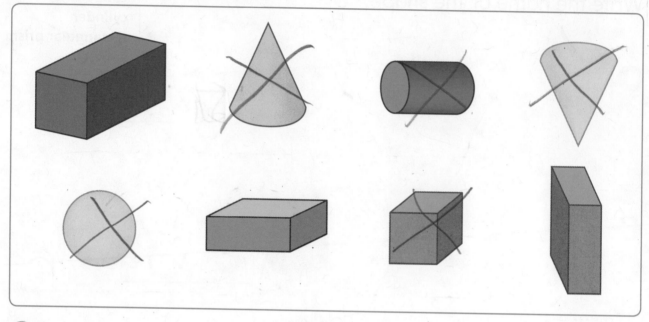

7 Ring the shapes that are **cubes**.

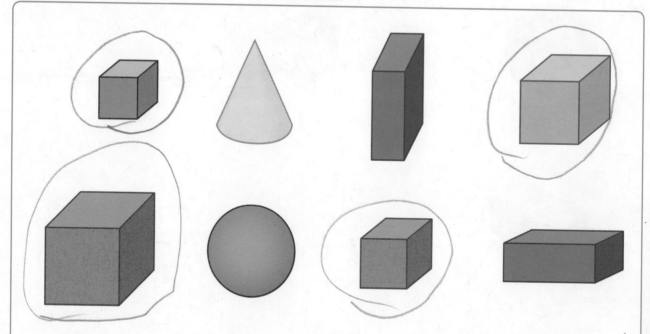

✓ **Check Understanding**
Compare a **cylinder**, a **cone**, and a
sphere. Explain what is the same and
different about the shapes.

3-Dimensional Shapes

Name _____

Ring the shapes used to make the new shape.

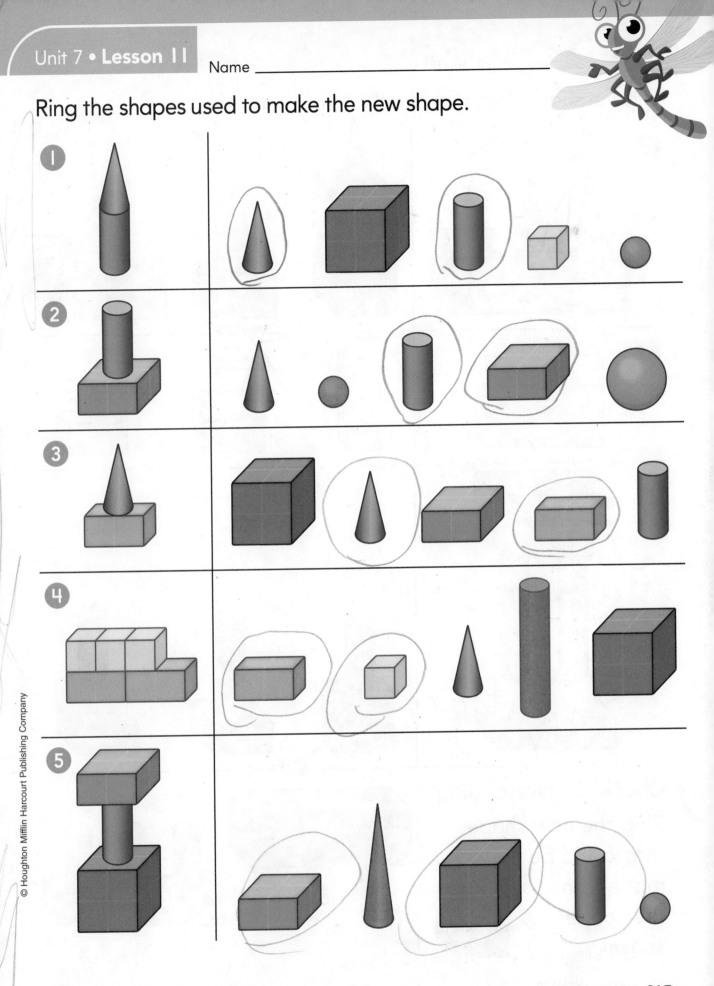

Ring the shape used to make the larger shape.

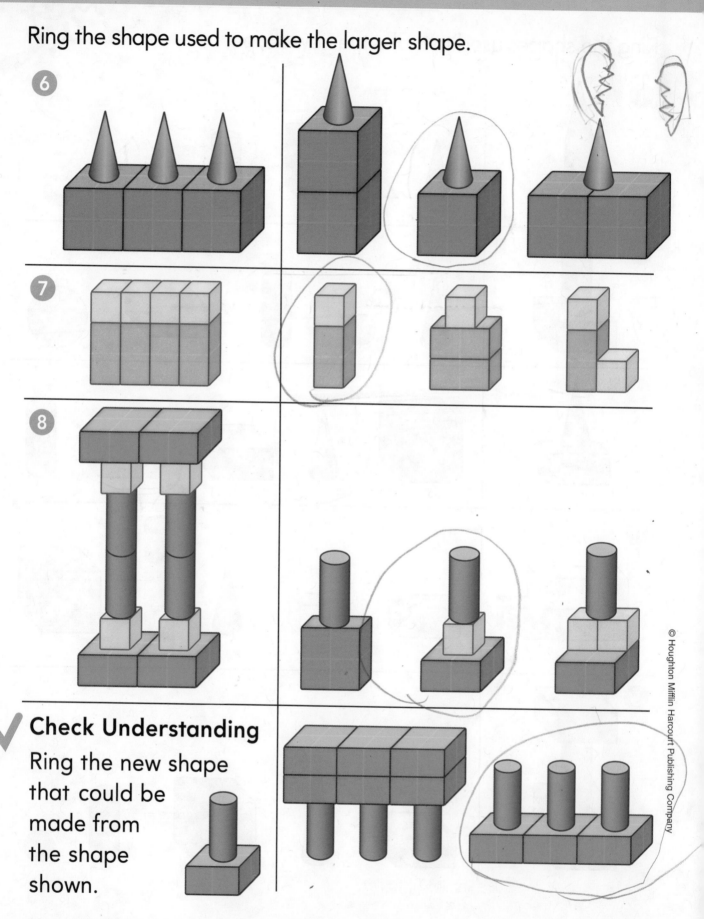

6

7

8

✓ **Check Understanding**

Ring the new shape that could be made from the shape shown.

Compose 3-Dimensional Shapes

Name _____ Date _____

1 Draw an X on the shape that is NOT a square.

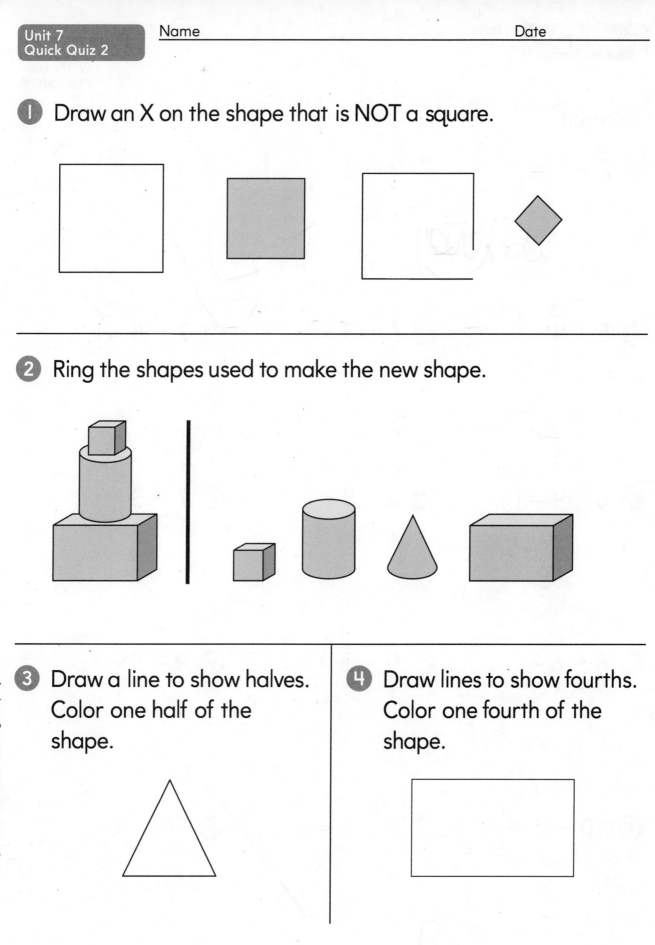

2 Ring the shapes used to make the new shape.

3 Draw a line to show halves.
Color one half of the
shape.

4 Draw lines to show fourths.
Color one fourth of the
shape.

Name _____   Date _____

Subtract.

1 2 − 1 = ☐   **2** 4 − 2 = ☐   **3** 3 − 0 = ☐

4 5 − 4 = ☐   **5** 6 − 3 = ☐   **6** 7 − 5 = ☐

7 6 − 4 = ☐   **8** 8 − 8 = ☐   **9** 7 − 3 = ☐

10 8 − 6 = ☐   **11** 9 − 2 = ☐   **12** 9 − 5 = ☐

13 10 − 8 = ☐   **14** 8 − 3 = ☐   **15** 10 − 4 = ☐

Write 1, 2, 3 to order from **shortest** to **longest**.

VOCABULARY
shortest
longest

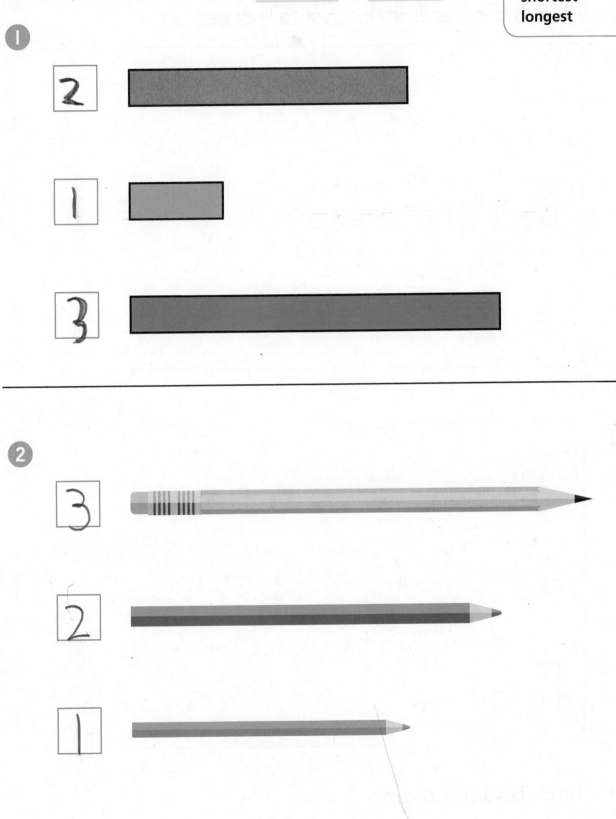

1

2

1

3

2

3

2

1

Draw three lines of different lengths.
Write 1, 2, 3 to order from longest to shortest.

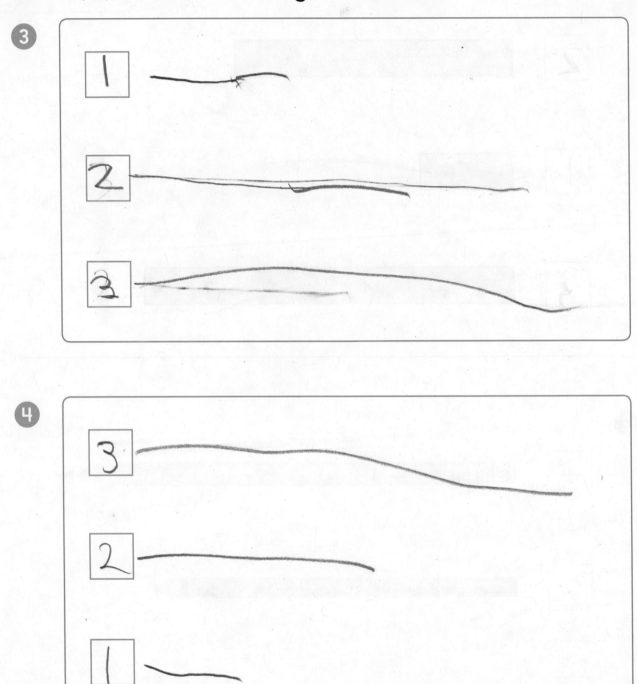

3

1

2

3

4

3

2

1

✓ Check Understanding

Explain how to put 3 lengths in order.

Order by Length

Jay and his family are going on a picnic.
Draw lines to show equal shares.

① Jay wants to share his burger
with his mom. How can he cut
his burger into two equal shares?

② Jay and his three sisters want
to share a pan of corn bread.
How can he cut the bread into
four equal shares?

③ Jay's mom and his three
sisters want to share a block of
cheese. How can they cut the
block of cheese into four
equal shares?

There will be lots of food at the picnic.
Measure the food in small paper clips.

4 Orange slice   How long? ☐ paper clips

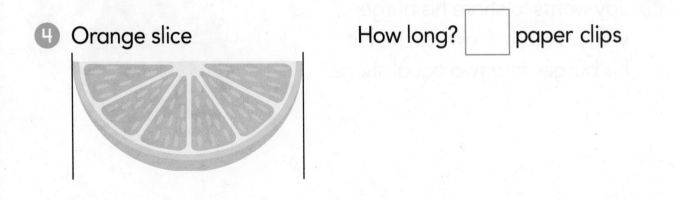

5 Celery   How long? ☐ paper clips

6 Cracker   How long? ☐ paper clips

7 Order the picnic food from longest
to shortest. Write the names.

_____

Focus on Mathematical Practices

Name _____ Date _____

Write 1, 2, 3 to order from longest to shortest.

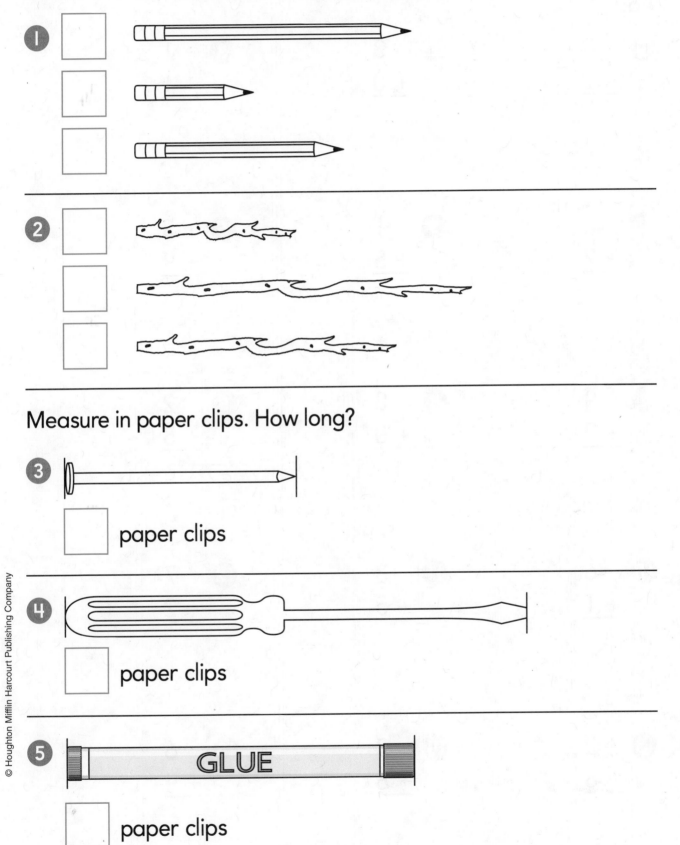

1

2

Measure in paper clips. How long?

3 [ ] paper clips

4 [ ] paper clips

5 GLUE

[ ] paper clips

Name _____ Date _____

PATH to FLUENCY

Add.

1) 0
   + 1
   ___

2) 3
   + 0
   ___

3) 1
   + 1
   ___

4) 2
   + 2
   ___

5) 1
   + 5
   ___

6) 3
   + 4
   ___

7) 4
   + 2
   ___

8) 8
   + 0
   ___

9) 2
   + 5
   ___

10) 6
    + 1
    ___

11) 3
    + 5
    ___

12) 7
    + 2
    ___

13) 2
    + 8
    ___

14) 3
    + 6
    ___

15) 6
    + 4
    ___

Read the clock.

Write the time on the digital clock.

① 7:00

② 4:30

Draw the hands to show the time.

③ 8:30

④ 3:00

⑤ Which shapes are NOT triangles?

Draw an X on each one.

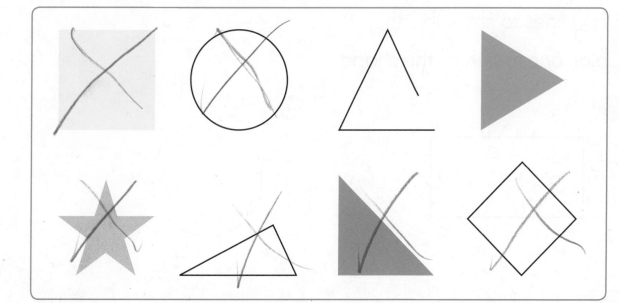

6 Is the shape a square? Choose Yes or No.

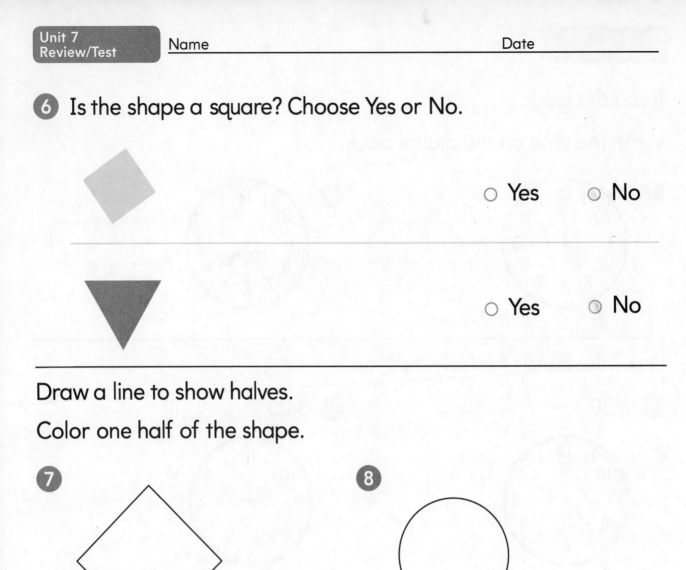

○ Yes   ⊙ No

○ Yes   ⊙ No

Draw a line to show halves.

Color one half of the shape.

7

8

Draw lines to show fourths.

Color one fourth of the shape.

9

10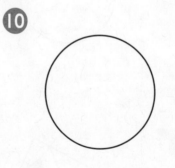

11 Draw a line from the shape to its name.

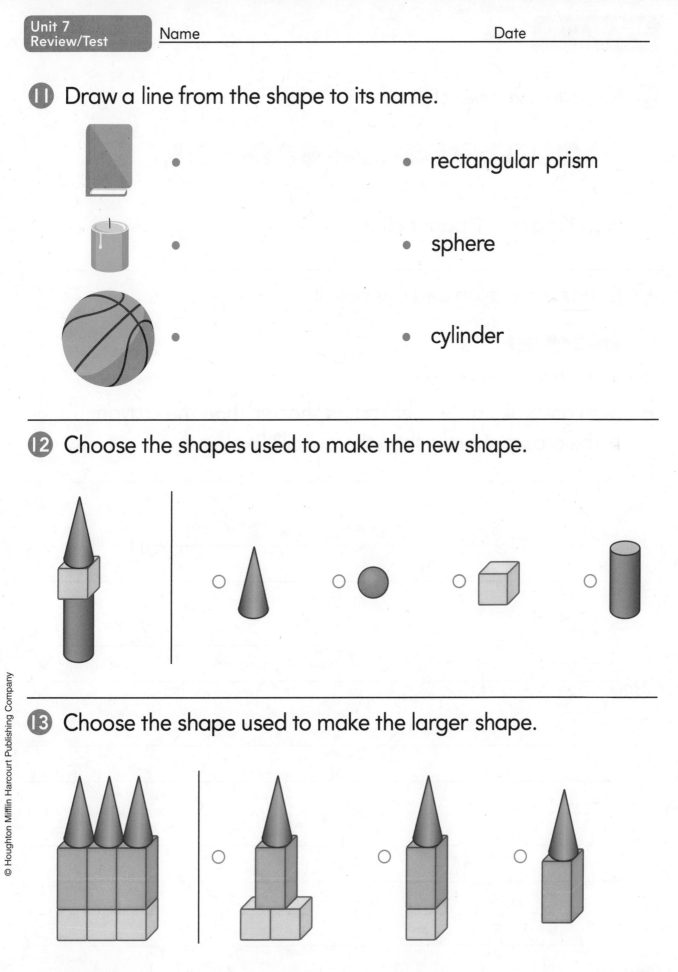

• rectangular prism

• sphere

• cylinder

12 Choose the shapes used to make the new shape.

13 Choose the shape used to make the larger shape.

14 Measure in paper clips.

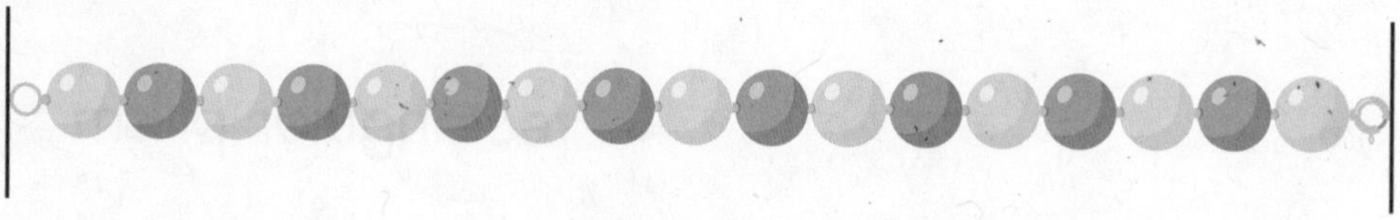

How long? ☐ paper clips

15 Eli has this crayon and this pencil.

Sam gives him an eraser that is shorter than the crayon.
Is the eraser shorter than the pencil? Explain.

Yes. The eraser
is shorter

Busy Bug's Day

1 **Part A**

The clock hands show Busy Bug's bedtime.

Write the same time on the digital clock.

Part B Tell how you know what time it is.

2 **Part A** This is the shape of Busy Bug's snack.

He wants to share his snack with three friends.

Draw lines to show fourths.

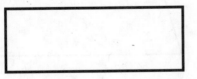

Part B Tell how you know the parts are fourths.

Busy Bug's Day (continued)

3 **Part A** Busy Bug likes only squares. Help him find the squares. Draw an X on each shape that is NOT a square.

Part B Tell how you know a shape is a square.

4 **Part A**

This is Busy Bug's walking stick.

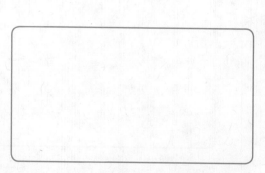

This is Busy Bug's bed.

How many paper clips long is the bed?

_____

Part B

Busy Bug's table is longer than his walking stick. It is shorter than his bed. Draw Busy Bug's table.

Dear Family:

Your child will be using special drawings of 10-sticks and circles to add greater numbers. The sticks show the number of tens, and the circles show the number of ones. When a new group of ten is made, a ring is drawn around it.

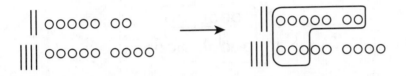

There are several ways for children to show the new group of ten when they add 2-digit numbers.

- Children can do the addition with a single total. The 1 for the new ten can be written either below the tens column or above it. Writing it below makes addition easier because the 1 new ten is added after children have added the two numbers that are already there. Also, children can see the 16 they made from 7 and 9 because the 1 and 6 are closer together than they were when the new ten was written above.

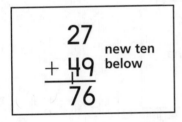

- Children can make separate totals for tens and ones. Many first-graders prefer to work from left to right because that is how they read. They add the tens (20 + 40 = 60) and then the ones (7 + 9 = 16). The last step is to add the two totals together (60 + 16 = 76).

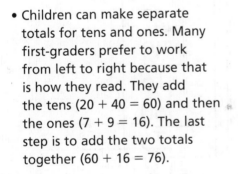

left to right   right to left

You may notice your child using one of these methods as he or she completes homework.

Sincerely,
Your child's teacher

CC SS Unit 8 addresses the following standards from the Common Core State Standards for Mathematics: **1.OA.C.6, 1.NBT.B.2, 1.NBT.B.2.a, 1.NBT.B.2.c, 1.NBT.B.3, 1.NBT.C.4, 1.NBT.C.6, and all** Mathematical Practices.

Estimada familia:

Su niño usará dibujos especiales de palitos de decenas y círculos para sumar números más grandes. Los palitos muestran el número de decenas y los círculos muestran el número de unidades. Cuando se forma un nuevo grupo de diez, se encierra.

Hay varias maneras en las que los niños pueden mostrar el nuevo grupo de diez al sumar números de 2 dígitos.

- Pueden hacer la suma con un total único. El 1 que indica la nueva decena se puede escribir abajo o arriba de la columna de las decenas. Escribirlo abajo hace que la suma sea más fácil porque la nueva decena se suma después de sumar los dos números que ya estaban allí. Además, los niños pueden ver el 16 que obtuvieron de 7 y 9 porque el 1 y el 6 están más juntos que cuando la nueva decena estaba escrita arriba.

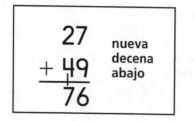

- Pueden hacer totales separados para decenas y para unidades. Muchos estudiantes de primer grado prefieren trabajar de izquierda a derecha porque así leen. Suman las decenas (20 + 40 = 60) y luego las unidades (7 + 9 = 16). El último paso es sumar ambos totales (60 + 16 = 76).

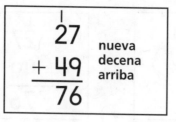

de izquierda a derecha   de derecha a izquierda

Es posible que su niño use uno de estos métodos al hacer la tarea.

Atentamente,
El maestro de su niño

© Houghton Mifflin Harcourt Publishing Company

CC SS En la Unidad 8 se aplican los siguientes estándares de los Estándares estatales comunes de matemáticas: 1.OA.C.6, 1.NBT.B.2, 1.NBT.B.2.a, 1.NBT.B.2.c, 1.NBT.C.3, 1.NBT.C.4, 1.NBT.C.6 y todos los de Prácticas matemáticas.

Draw circles to show the apples.

Uncle David
28 Apples

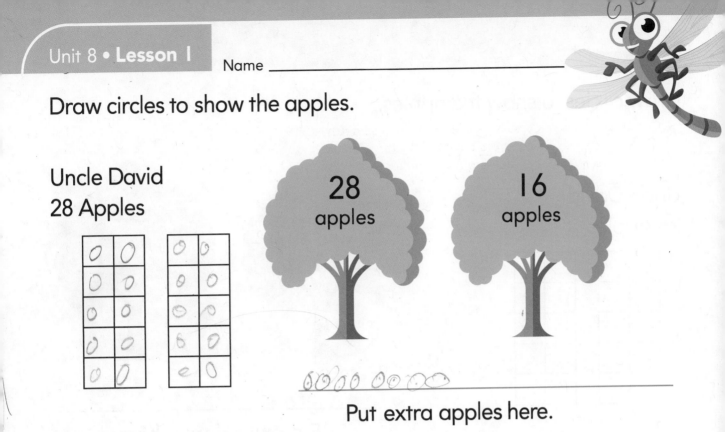

28
apples

16
apples

Put extra apples here.

Aunt Sarah
16 Apples

Put extra apples here.

Total Apples

tens tens

4 4

Put extra apples here.

Draw circles to show the apples.

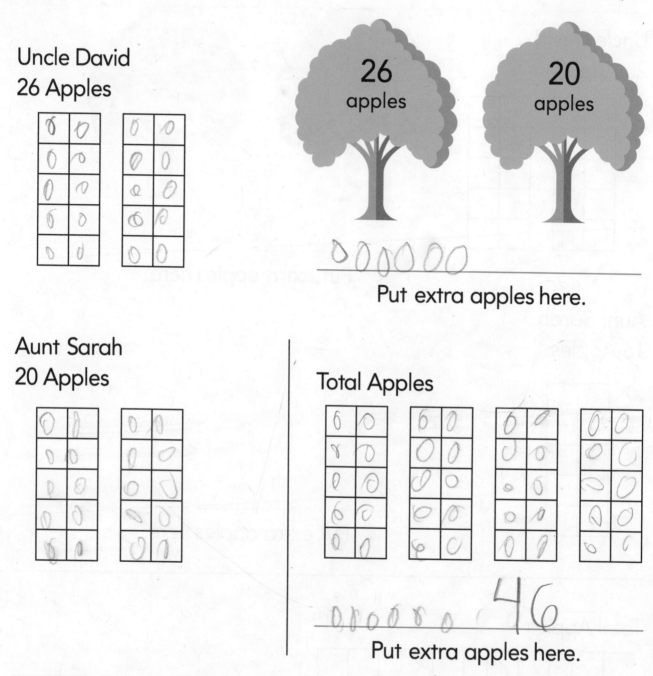

Uncle David
26 Apples

26 apples

20 apples

Put extra apples here.

Aunt Sarah
20 Apples

Total Apples

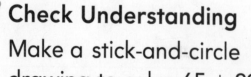

Put extra apples here.

✔ **Check Understanding**
Make a stick-and-circle
drawing to solve 65 + 29.

Explore 2-Digit Addition

Name _____

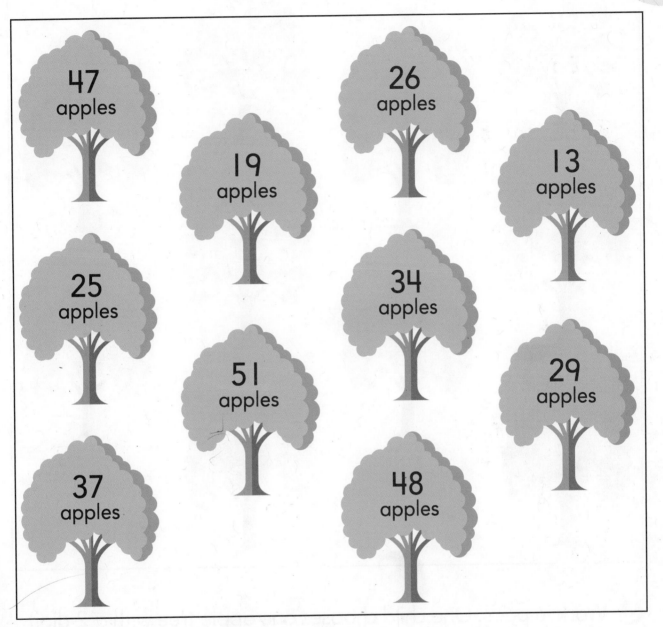

① Work in pairs. Each child chooses one apple tree.

② On your MathBoard or paper, add the number of apples in the two trees.

③ Check to see if you both got the same answer.

④ Repeat with other trees.

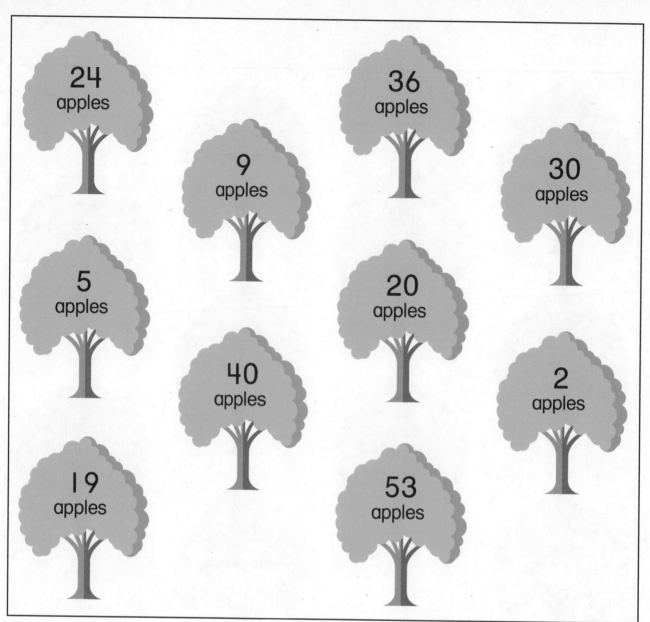

5 Work in pairs. One child chooses one apple tree with a 2-digit number. The other child chooses another tree.

6 On your MathBoard or paper, add the apples in the two trees.

7 Check to see if you both got the same answer.

✓ **Check Understanding**

Use the New Group Below method to solve 55 + 36.

Methods of 2-Digit Addition

Name _____

Write the numbers to show addition.

1

30 6
3 **6** ⟶ 30 **3 0** + 6 **6**

50 5
5 **5** ⟶ 50 **5 0** + 5 **5**

$$36 = 30 + 6$$
$$\underline{+\ 55 = 50 + 5}$$

$$\boxed{} + \boxed{} = \boxed{}$$

2

50 4
5 **4** ⟶ 50 **5 0** + 4 **4**

30 8
3 **8** ⟶ 30 **3 0** + 8 **8**

$$54 = 50 + 4$$
$$\underline{+\ 38 = 30 + 8}$$

$$\boxed{} + \boxed{} = \boxed{}$$

CC SS Content Standards **1.NBT.C.4**
Mathematical Practices **MP3, MP4, MP5, MP6**

Write the numbers to show addition.

3 Mark built a tower using 67 blocks. Elizabeth built a tower using 18 blocks. How many blocks did they use together?

Step 1: Add the tens.

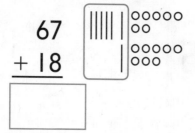

```
  67
+ 18
┌──────┐
│      │
└──────┘
```

Step 2: Add the ones.

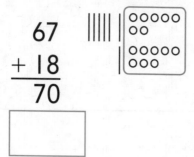

```
  67
+ 18
  70
┌──────┐
│      │
└──────┘
```

Step 3: Add the totals together.

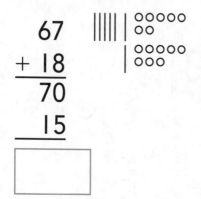

```
  67
+ 18
  70
  15
┌──────┐
│      │
└──────┘
```

✓ **Check Understanding**

Use the Show All Totals method and make a Proof Drawing to solve 63 + 28.

Addition of Tens and Ones

Name _____

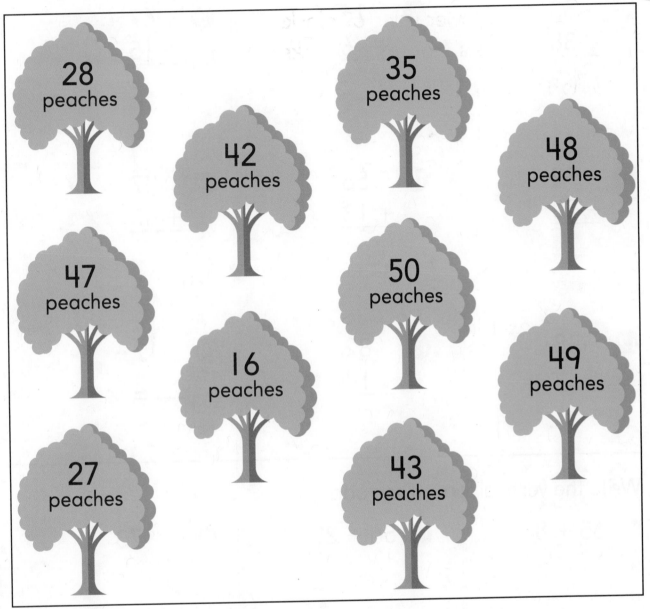

① Work in pairs. Each child chooses one peach tree.

② On your MathBoard or paper, add the number of peaches in the two trees.

③ Check to see if you both got the same answer.

④ Repeat with other trees.

⑤ For which problems did you make a new ten?

Add.

6
$$
\begin{array}{r}
\overset{1}{5}3 \\
+\ 38 \\
\hline
91
\end{array}
$$

7
$$
\begin{array}{r}
\overset{1}{1}6 \\
+\ \ 6 \\
\hline
22
\end{array}
$$

8
$$
\begin{array}{r}
\overset{1}{6}7 \\
+\ 15 \\
\hline
82
\end{array}
$$

9
$$
\begin{array}{r}
\overset{1}{7}2 \\
+\ 20 \\
\hline
92
\end{array}
$$

10
$$
\begin{array}{r}
\overset{1}{5}6 \\
+\ 13 \\
\hline
69
\end{array}
$$

11
$$
\begin{array}{r}
\overset{1}{4}7 \\
+\ 30 \\
\hline
87
\end{array}
$$

12
$$
\begin{array}{r}
\overset{1}{4}8 \\
+\ \ 5 \\
\hline
\end{array}
$$

13
$$
\begin{array}{r}
\overset{1}{8}2 \\
+\ 14 \\
\hline
\end{array}
$$

14
$$
\begin{array}{r}
\overset{1}{1}7 \\
+\ \ 2 \\
\hline
\end{array}
$$

Write the vertical form. Then add.

15 65 + 8

16 56 + 28

17 6 + 73

✔ Check Understanding

Use two different methods to solve 15 + 18.

Discuss Solution Methods

Name _____

Add.

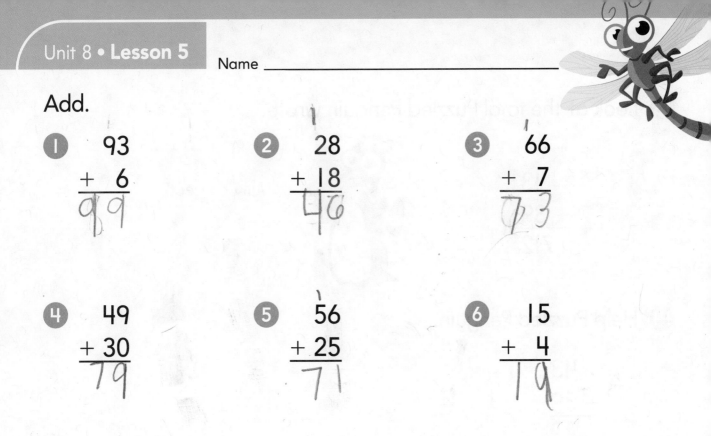

1   93
    + 6
    99

2   28
    + 18
    46

3   66
    + 7
    73

4   49
    + 30
    79

5   56
    + 25
    71

6   15
    + 4
    19

Write the vertical form. Then add.

7 71 + 19 = 90
    71
  + 19
    90

8 54 + 20 = 74
    54
  + 20
    84

9 33 + 29 = 62
    33
  + 29
    72

10 44 + 4 = 48
    44
  + 4
    48

11 8 + 74 = 82
    74
  + 8
    82

12 19 + 67 = 86
    67
  + 19
    86

CCSS Content Standards **1.OA.C.6, 1.NBT.C.4**
Mathematical Practices **MP3, MP6**

13 Look at the total Puzzled Penguin wrote.

$$\begin{array}{r} 43 \\ + 39 \\ \hline 712 \end{array}$$

Am I correct?

NO Xoq

14 Help Puzzled Penguin.

$$\begin{array}{r} 43 \\ + 39 \\ \hline 82 \end{array}$$

PATH to FLUENCY Add.

1 $5 + 2 = \boxed{7}$

2 $7 + 1 = \boxed{8}$

3 $3 + 2 = \boxed{5}$

4 $\boxed{10} = 8 + 2$

5 $\boxed{9} = 3 + 6$

6 $\boxed{7} = 4 + 3$

7 $5 + 1 = \boxed{6}$

8 $6 + 2 = \boxed{8}$

9 $5 + 3 = \boxed{8}$

10 $\boxed{9} = 7 + 2$

11 $\boxed{6} = 4 + 2$

12 $\boxed{3} = 2 + 1$

✔ **Check Understanding**

Write $26 + 18$ as a vertical form and solve.

Practice 2-Digit Addition

Use the pictures to solve. Show your work.

1 How many potatoes are there?

49 potatoes

47 potatoes

☐ potatoes

2 How many cartons of milk are there?

37 cartons of milk

23 cartons of milk

☐ cartons of milk

3 20 cartons of milk spill.
How many cartons of milk are there now?

☐ cartons of milk

© Houghton Mifflin Harcourt Publishing Company • Image Credits: ©asiseeit/Getty Images

Use the pictures to solve. Show your work.

4 How many jars of honey are there?

 jars of honey

5 How many jars of jam are there?

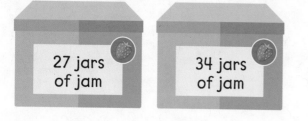

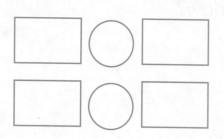

jars of jam

6 Compare the number of jars of honey to the number of jars of jam. Write the comparison 2 ways.

Focus on Mathematical Practices

Unit 8
Quick Quiz 1

Name ______________________ Date ______________

Add.

1
$$\begin{array}{r} 27 \\ +\ \ 5 \\ \hline \end{array}$$

2
$$\begin{array}{r} 43 \\ +\ 30 \\ \hline \end{array}$$

3
$$\begin{array}{r} 58 \\ +\ 26 \\ \hline \end{array}$$

Write the vertical form. Then add.

4 $29 + 34$

5 $38 + 6$

Name _____ Date _____

Add.

1 2 + 2 = ☐   2 3 + 3 = ☐   3 1 + 3 = ☐

4 3 + 2 = ☐   5 4 + 3 = ☐   6 1 + 7 = ☐

7 2 + 4 = ☐   8 4 + 6 = ☐   9 6 + 2 = ☐

10 7 + 2 = ☐   11 5 + 4 = ☐   12 7 + 3 = ☐

13 ☐ = 3 + 5   14 ☐ = 2 + 8   15 ☐ = 5 + 4

Solve. Group ones to make tens.

1 Grace has 18 apples.   Jake has 24 apples.

  extra apples

 extra apples

How many apples do they have?

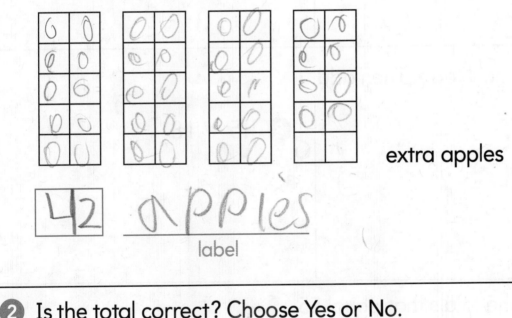 extra apples

42 apples
    label

---

2 Is the total correct? Choose Yes or No.

$45 + 20 = 47$ ○ Yes   ● No

$30 + 25 = 55$ ● Yes   ○ No

$79 + 10 = 89$ ● Yes   ○ No

$14 + 50 = 74$ ○ Yes   ● No

Add.

③
```
   1
  63
+ 29
─────
  92
```

④
```
  52
+ 20
─────
  72
```

⑤
```
   1
  78
+  5
─────
  83
```

⑥
```
   1
  26
+ 15
─────
  31
```

Write the vertical form. Then add.

⑦ 28 + 9
```
  28
+  9
─────
  37
```

⑧ 45 + 18
```
  45
+ 18
─────
  53
```

⑨ Choose the totals that equal 55.

⦿ 51 + 4   ⦿ 46 + 9   ○ 34 + 22   ⦿ 35 + 20

⑩ Choose the totals that equal 84.

○ 35 + 49   ⦿ 34 + 44   ⦿ 42 + 42   ○ 50 + 34

11 How many apples are there?
Show your work.

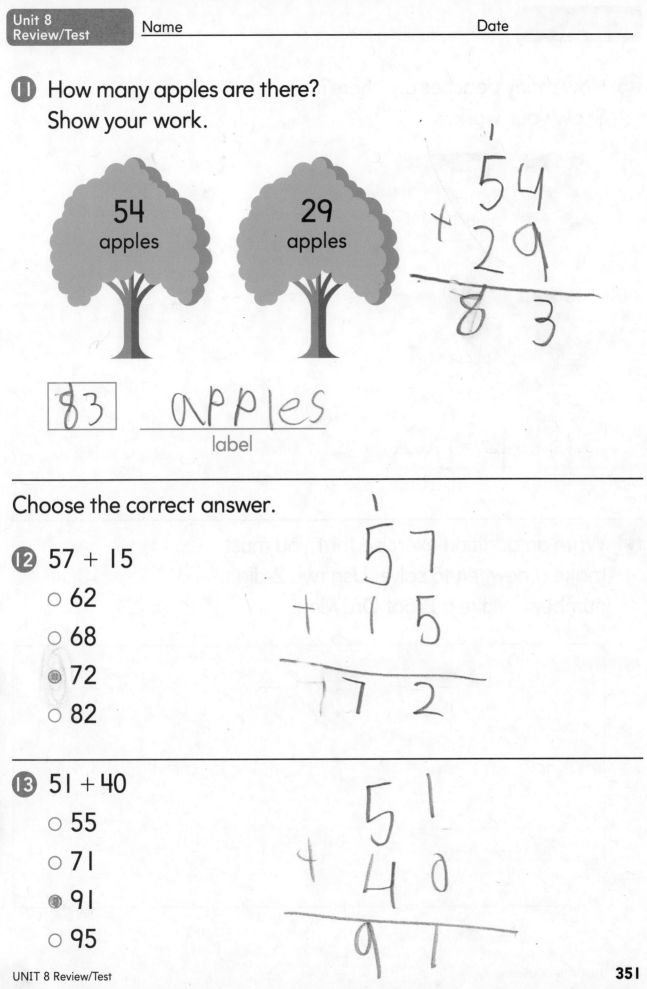

54
apples

29
apples

$\begin{array}{r} \overset{1}{54} \\ + 29 \\ \hline 83 \end{array}$

83 apples
       label

Choose the correct answer.

12 57 + 15

$\begin{array}{r} \overset{1}{57} \\ + 15 \\ \hline 72 \end{array}$

○ 62
○ 68
◉ 72
○ 82

13 51 + 40

$\begin{array}{r} 51 \\ + 40 \\ \hline 91 \end{array}$

○ 55
○ 71
◉ 91
○ 95

⑭ How many peaches are there?
Show your work.

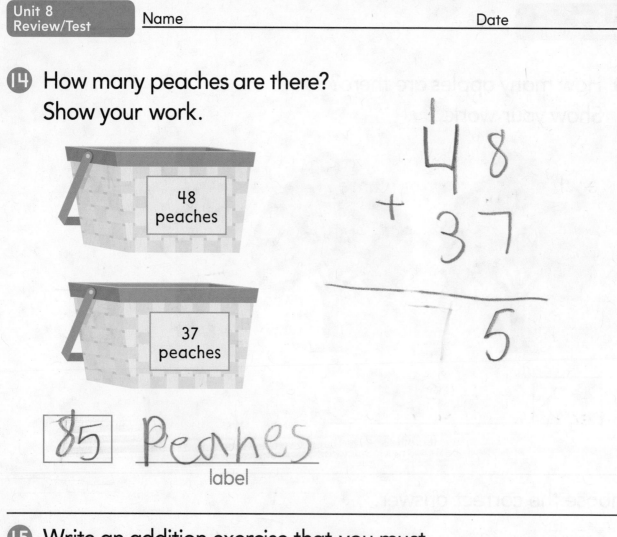

48
peaches

37
peaches

$$
\begin{array}{r}
\overset{1}{4}\,8 \\
+\ 3\,7 \\
\hline
7\,5
\end{array}
$$

⎡85⎤ Peahes
 ‾‾‾‾‾‾‾‾‾‾‾
 label

⑮ Write an addition exercise that you must
make a new ten to solve. Use two 2-digit
numbers. Make a Proof Drawing.

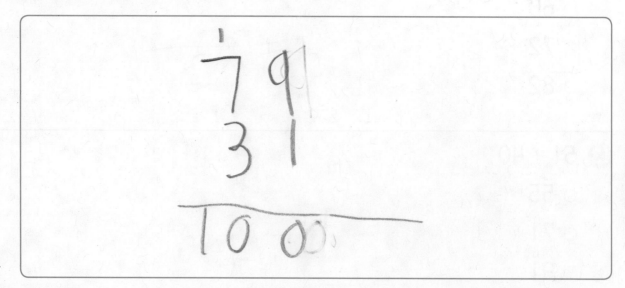

$$
\begin{array}{r}
\overset{1}{7}\,9 \\
3\,1 \\
\hline
1\,0\,0
\end{array}
$$

Name _____

How Many Pears?

Some friends pick pears.

Choose one of the numbers below for each $\bigcirc$.
Use each number only one time.

9   16   27   35

1 Lisa picks more pears than Rena.
Together they pick 36 pears.
How many does each girl pick?

Lisa picks $\bigcirc$ pears.

Rena picks $\bigcirc$ pears.

Show how you know.

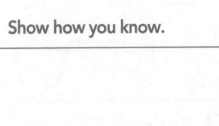

---

2 Luis and Tran pick $\bigcirc$ pears.
Then they pick 20 more pears.
What is the total number of
pears they pick?

☐ pears

Show how you know.

---

3 Maya picks $\bigcirc$ pears. Vinny
picks 15 pears. How many
pears do they pick in all?

☐ pears

Show how you know.

How Many Pears? (continued)

4 Jamal picks 38 pears.
His grandma picks 24 pears.
How many pears do they
pick altogether?

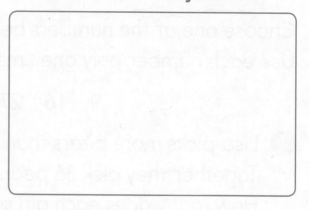

Show and tell how you know.

☐ pears

5 Kat picks 25 pears. Alex picks
19 pears. They want to find how
many pears they pick altogether.
Look at the total.

$$
\begin{array}{r}
25 \\
+\ 19 \\
\hline
\cancel{314} \\
\end{array}
$$

Tell why the total is not correct.
Find the correct total.

Addition and Subtraction Problem Types

	Result Unknown	Change Unknown	Start Unknown
Add To	Six children are playing tag in the yard. Three more children come to play. How many children are playing in the yard now? *Situation and Solution Equation[1]:* $6 + 3 = \square$	Six children are playing tag in the yard. Some more children come to play. Now there are 9 children in the yard. How many children came to play? *Situation Equation:* $6 + \square = 9$ *Solution Equation:* $9 - 6 = \square$	Some children are playing tag in the yard. Three more children come to play. Now there are 9 children in the yard. How many children were in the yard at first? *Situation Equation:* $\square + 3 = 9$ *Solution Equation:* $9 - 3 = \square$
Take From	Jake has 10 trading cards. He gives 3 to his brother. How many trading cards does he have left? *Situation and Solution Equation:* $10 - 3 = \square$	Jake has 10 trading cards. He gives some to his brother. Now Jake has 7 trading cards left. How many cards does he give to his brother? *Situation Equation:* $10 - \square = 7$ *Solution Equation:* $10 - 7 = \square$	Jake has some trading cards. He gives 3 to his brother. Now Jake has 7 trading cards left. How many cards does he start with? *Situation Equation:* $\square - 3 = 7$ *Solution Equation:* $7 + 3 = \square$

[1]A situation equation represents the structure (action) in the problem situation. A solution equation shows the operation used to find the answer.

Addition and Subtraction Problem Types (continued)

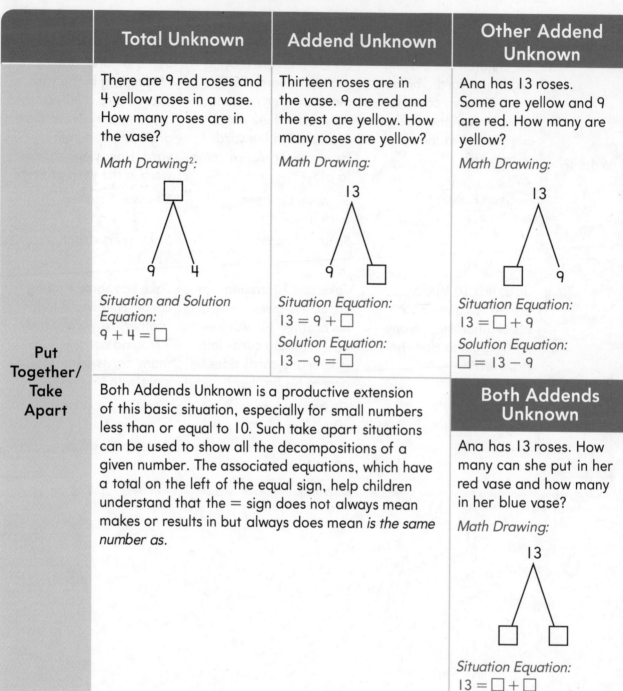

	Total Unknown	Addend Unknown	Other Addend Unknown
Put Together/ Take Apart	There are 9 red roses and 4 yellow roses in a vase. How many roses are in the vase? *Math Drawing²:* 9 4 *Situation and Solution Equation:* $9 + 4 = \square$	Thirteen roses are in the vase. 9 are red and the rest are yellow. How many roses are yellow? *Math Drawing:* 13 9 $\square$ *Situation Equation:* $13 = 9 + \square$ *Solution Equation:* $13 - 9 = \square$	Ana has 13 roses. Some are yellow and 9 are red. How many are yellow? *Math Drawing:* 13 $\square$ 9 *Situation Equation:* $13 = \square + 9$ *Solution Equation:* $\square = 13 - 9$

Both Addends Unknown is a productive extension of this basic situation, especially for small numbers less than or equal to 10. Such take apart situations can be used to show all the decompositions of a given number. The associated equations, which have a total on the left of the equal sign, help children understand that the $=$ sign does not always mean makes or results in but always does mean *is the same number as.*

Both Addends Unknown

Ana has 13 roses. How many can she put in her red vase and how many in her blue vase?

Math Drawing:

13
$\square$ $\square$

Situation Equation:
$13 = \square + \square$

²These math drawings are called Math Mountains in Grades 1–3 and break-apart drawings in Grades 4 and 5.

Addition and Subtraction Problem Types (continued)

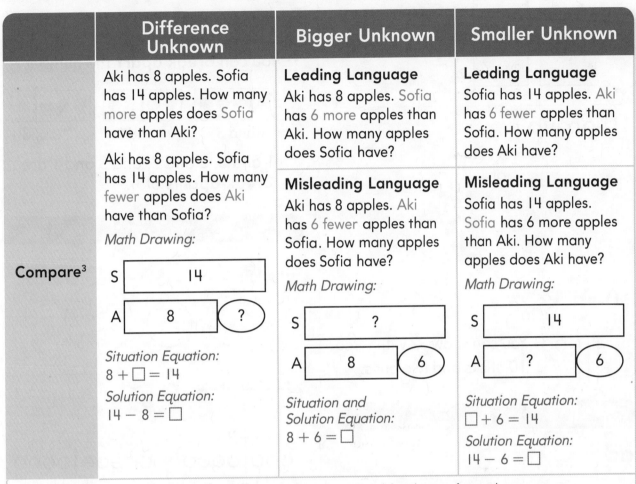

	Difference Unknown	Bigger Unknown	Smaller Unknown
Compare[3]	Aki has 8 apples. Sofia has 14 apples. How many more apples does Sofia have than Aki? Aki has 8 apples. Sofia has 14 apples. How many fewer apples does Aki have than Sofia? *Math Drawing:* S | 14 | A | 8 | ? *Situation Equation:* $8 + \square = 14$ *Solution Equation:* $14 - 8 = \square$	**Leading Language** Aki has 8 apples. Sofia has 6 more apples than Aki. How many apples does Sofia have? **Misleading Language** Aki has 8 apples. Aki has 6 fewer apples than Sofia. How many apples does Sofia have? *Math Drawing:* S | ? | A | 8 | 6 *Situation and Solution Equation:* $8 + 6 = \square$	**Leading Language** Sofia has 14 apples. Aki has 6 fewer apples than Sofia. How many apples does Aki have? **Misleading Language** Sofia has 14 apples. Sofia has 6 more apples than Aki. How many apples does Aki have? *Math Drawing:* S | 14 | A | ? | 6 *Situation Equation:* $\square + 6 = 14$ *Solution Equation:* $14 - 6 = \square$

[3]A comparison sentence can always be said in two ways. One way uses *more*, and the other uses *fewer* or *less*. Misleading language suggests the wrong operation. For example, it says *Aki has 6 fewer apples than Sofia*, but you have to add 6 to Aki's 8 apples to get 14 apples.

5-group*

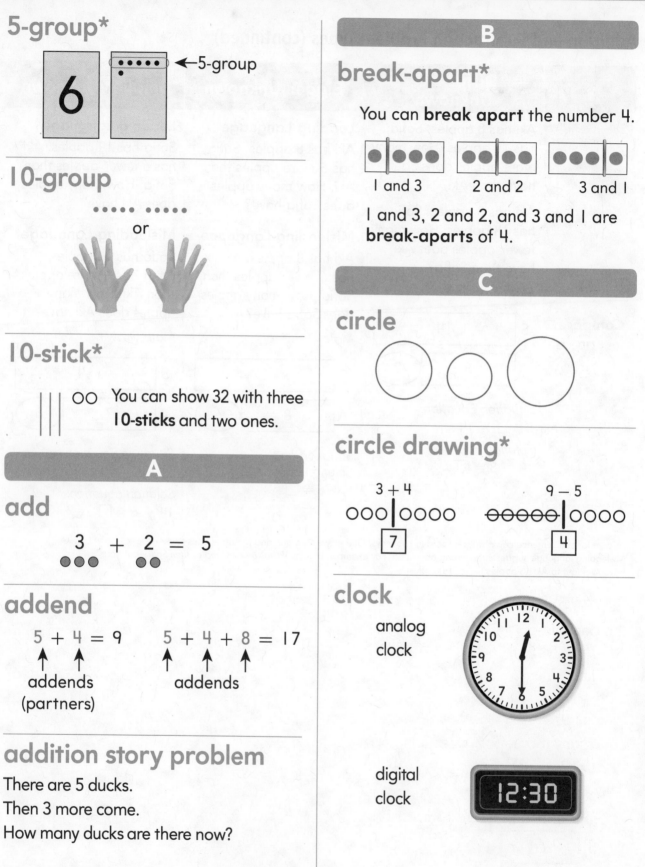

6   ····· ←—5-group

10-group

····· ·····

or

10-stick*

||| OO You can show 32 with three **10-sticks** and two ones.

add

3 + 2 = 5

addend

5 + 4 = 9   5 + 4 + 8 = 17

↑   ↑   ↑   ↑   ↑

addends   addends
(partners)

addition story problem

There are 5 ducks.

Then 3 more come.

How many ducks are there now?

break-apart*

You can **break apart** the number 4.

●|●●●   ●●|●●   ●●●|●
1 and 3   2 and 2   3 and 1

1 and 3, 2 and 2, and 3 and 1 are **break-aparts** of 4.

circle

circle drawing*

3 + 4   9 − 5
OOO|OOOO   ⊖⊖⊖⊖⊖|OOOO
7   4

clock

analog
clock

digital
clock

12:30

*A classroom research-based term developed for *Math Expressions*

column

1	11	21	31	41	51	61	71	81	91
2	12	22	32	42	52	62	72	82	92
3	13	23	33	43	53	63	73	83	93
4	14	24	34	44	54	64	74	84	94
5	15	25	35	45	55	65	75	85	95
6	16	26	36	46	56	66	76	86	96
7	17	27	37	47	57	67	77	87	97
8	18	28	38	48	58	68	78	88	98
9	19	29	39	49	59	69	79	89	99
10	20	30	40	50	60	70	80	90	100

compare

You can **compare** numbers.

11 is less than 12.

$11 < 12$

12 is greater than 11.

$12 > 11$

You can **compare** objects by length.

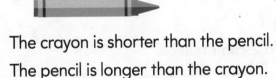

The crayon is shorter than the pencil.

The pencil is longer than the crayon.

comparison bars*

Joe has 6 roses. Sasha has 9 roses.
How many more roses does Sasha have
than Joe?

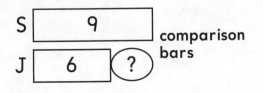

comparison bars

cone

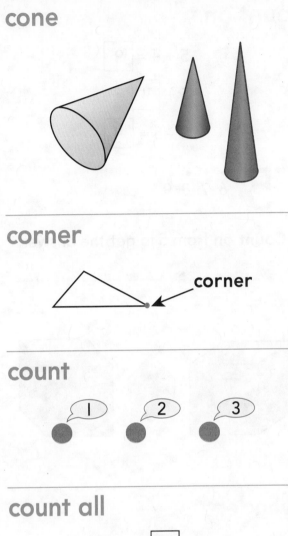

corner

corner

count

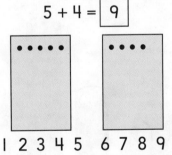

count all

$5 + 4 = \boxed{9}$

1 2 3 4 5   6 7 8 9

*A classroom research-based term developed for *Math Expressions*

count on

$$5 + 4 = \boxed{9}$$

$$5 + \boxed{4} = 9$$

$$9 - 5 = \boxed{4}$$

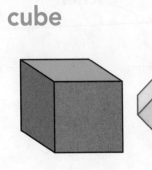

Count on from 5 to get the answer.

cube

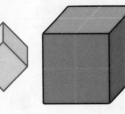

cylinder

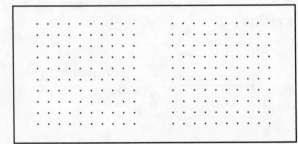

data

Colors in the Bag									
Red	◯	◯	◯						
Yellow	◯	◯	◯	◯	◯	◯	◯	◯	
Blue	◯	◯	◯	◯	◯	◯			

The **data** show how many of each color.

decade numbers

10, 20, 30, 40, 50, 60, 70, 80, 90

difference

$$11 - 3 = 8 \qquad \begin{array}{r} 11 \\ -3 \\ \hline 8 \end{array}$$

difference →

digit

15 is a 2-**digit** number.

The 1 in 15 means 1 ten.

The 5 in 15 means 5 ones.

Dot Array

*A classroom research-based term developed for *Math Expressions*

doubles

$$4 + 4 = 8$$

Both partners are the same.
They are doubles.

doubles minus 1

$7 + 7 = 14$, so
$7 + 6 = 13$, 1 less than 14.

doubles minus 2

$7 + 7 = 14$, so
$7 + 5 = 12$, 2 less than 14.

doubles plus 1

$6 + 6 = 12$, so
$6 + 7 = 13$, 1 more than 12.

doubles plus 2

$6 + 6 = 12$, so
$6 + 8 = 14$, 2 more than 12.

E

edge

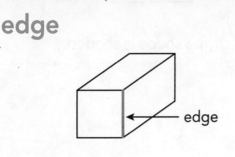
edge

equal shares

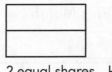

2 equal shares   4 equal shares

These show **equal shares.**

equal to (=)

$$4 + 4 = 8$$

4 plus 4 is **equal to** 8.

equation

Examples:

$$4 + 3 = 7 \qquad 7 = 4 + 3$$

$$9 - 5 = 4 \qquad 4 = 9 - 5$$

F

face

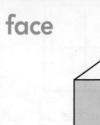
face

fewer

Eggs Laid This Month

Clucker laid **fewer** eggs than Vanilla.

fewest

Eggs Laid This Month

	Clucker	
Vanilla	
Daisy	

Clucker laid the **fewest** eggs.

---

fourth of

One **fourth of** the shape is shaded.

---

fourths

I whole

4 **fourths**, or
4 quarters

© Houghton Mifflin Harcourt Publishing Company

G

greater than (>)

|||° ° ° ° || ° ° ° ° °

34   >   25

34 is **greater than** 25.

---

grid

H

half-hour

minute
hand →

A **half-hour** is 30 minutes.

---

half of

One **half of** the shape is shaded.

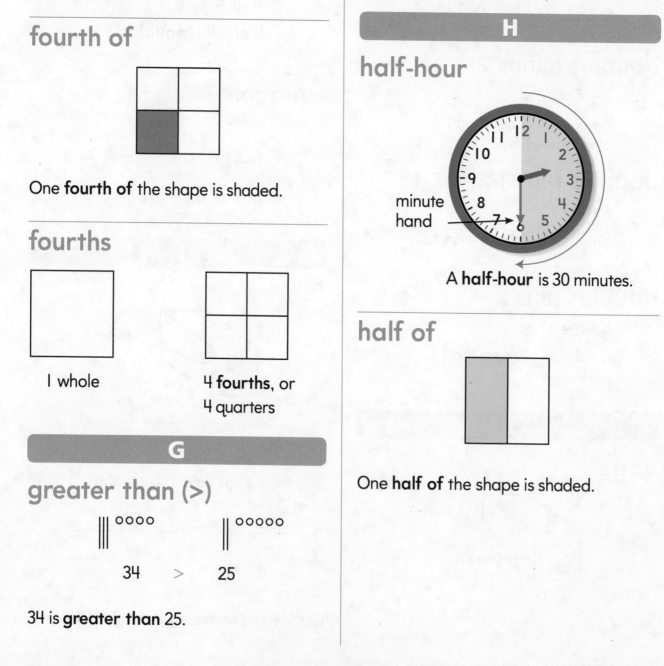

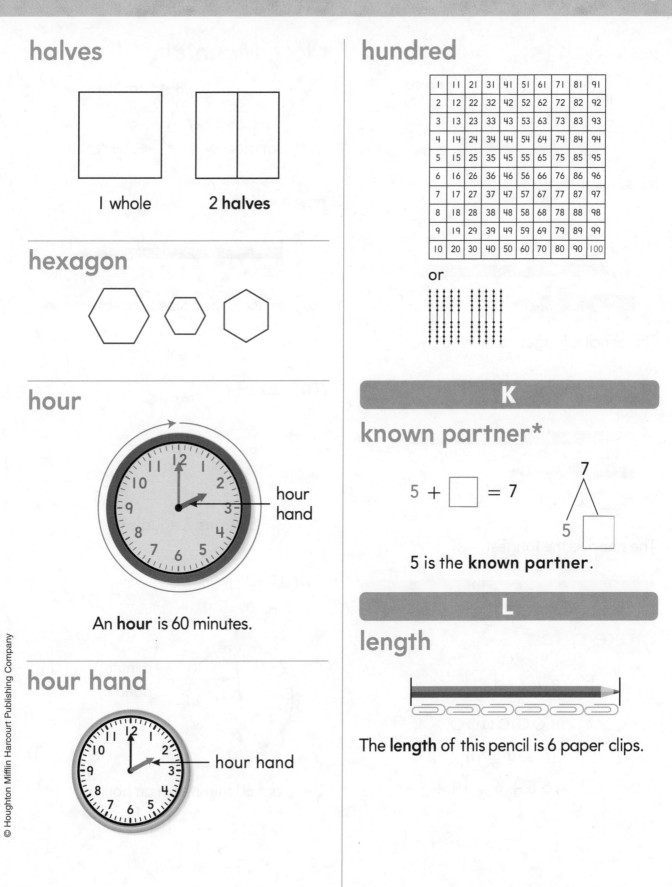

halves

I whole   2 **halves**

hexagon

hour

An **hour** is 60 minutes.

hour hand

hour hand

hour hand

hundred

1	11	21	31	41	51	61	71	81	91
2	12	22	32	42	52	62	72	82	92
3	13	23	33	43	53	63	73	83	93
4	14	24	34	44	54	64	74	84	94
5	15	25	35	45	55	65	75	85	95
6	16	26	36	46	56	66	76	86	96
7	17	27	37	47	57	67	77	87	97
8	18	28	38	48	58	68	78	88	98
9	19	29	39	49	59	69	79	89	99
10	20	30	40	50	60	70	80	90	100

or

K

known partner*

$5 + \boxed{} = 7$

7
5

5 is the **known partner**.

L

length

The **length** of this pencil is 6 paper clips.

*A classroom research-based term developed for *Math Expressions*

less than (<)

$$45 < 46$$

45 is **less than** 46.

longer

The pencil is **longer** than the crayon.

longest

The pencil is the **longest**.

make a ten

$$8 + 6 = \boxed{}$$

8 0 0 0 0 0 0

$$10 + 4 = 14,$$
so $8 + 6 = 14.$

Math Mountain*

8 ← total

partner → 5   3 ← partner

measure

You can use paper clips to **measure** the length of the pencil.

minus (−)

$$8 - 3 = 5 \qquad \begin{array}{r} 8 \\ -3 \\ \hline 5 \end{array}$$

8 **minus** 3 equals 5.

minute

I minute

minute hand

There are 60 **minutes** in an hour.

*A classroom research-based term developed for *Math Expressions*

more

Eggs Laid This Month

Clucker	● ● ● ●
Vanilla	○ ○ ○ ○ ○ ○ ○ ○ ○

Vanilla laid **more** eggs than Clucker.

most

Eggs Laid This Month

Clucker	● ● ● ●
Vanilla	○ ○ ○ ○ ○ ○ ○ ○ ○
Daisy	● ● ● ● ● ● ●

Vanilla laid the **most** eggs.

N

New Group Above Method*

$$\overset{1}{5}6$$
$$+\ 28$$
$$\overline{\ 84}$$

$6 + 8 = 14$
The 1 new ten in 14 goes up to the tens place.

New Group Below Method*

$$56$$
$$+\ 28$$
$$\overline{\ 84}$$

$6 + 8 = 14$
The 1 new ten in 14 goes below in the tens place.

not equal to (≠)

$$6 \neq 8$$

6 is **not equal to** 8.

number word

12

twelve ← number word

O

ones

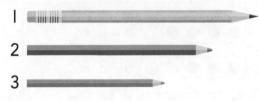

56 has 6 **ones**.

order

You can change the **order** of the partners.

$$7 + 2 = 9$$
$$2 + 7 = 9$$

You can **order** objects by length.

1
2
3

*A classroom research-based term developed for *Math Expressions*

Glossary

P

partner*

$$5 = 2 + 3$$

2 and 3 are **partners** of 5.
2 and 3 are 5-**partners**.

partner house*

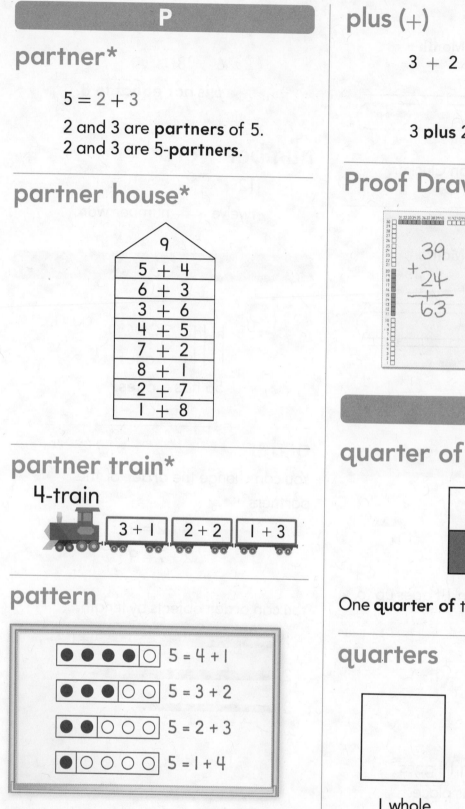

9
5 + 4
6 + 3
3 + 6
4 + 5
7 + 2
8 + 1
2 + 7
1 + 8

partner train*

4-train

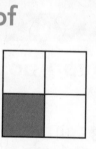

| 3 + 1 | 2 + 2 | 1 + 3 |

pattern

●●●●○	5 = 4 + 1
●●●○○	5 = 3 + 2
●●○○○	5 = 2 + 3
●○○○○	5 = 1 + 4

The partners of a number show a
pattern.

plus (+)

$$3 + 2 = 5 \qquad \begin{array}{r} 3 \\ + 2 \\ \hline 5 \end{array}$$

3 **plus** 2 equals 5.

Proof Drawing*

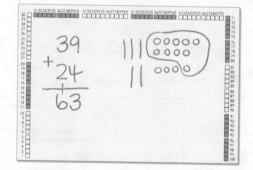

Q

quarter of

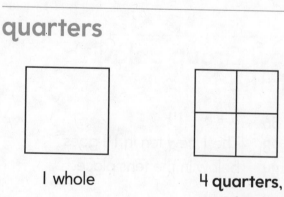

One **quarter of** the shape is shaded.

quarters

1 whole

4 **quarters**,
or 4 fourths

*A classroom research-based term developed for *Math Expressions*

R

rectangle

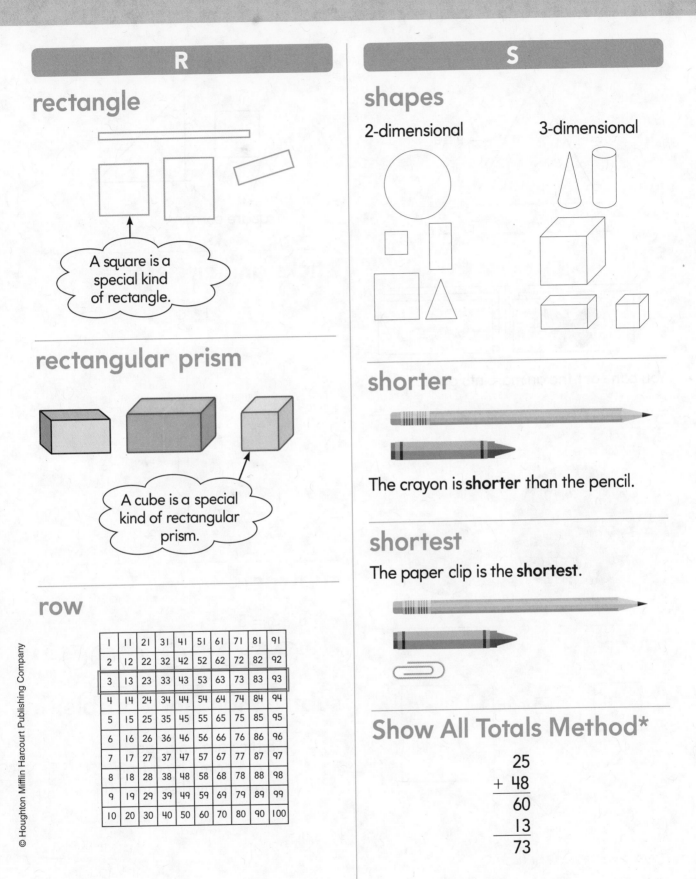

A square is a special kind of rectangle.

rectangular prism

A cube is a special kind of rectangular prism.

row

1	11	21	31	41	51	61	71	81	91
2	12	22	32	42	52	62	72	82	92
3	13	23	33	43	53	63	73	83	93
4	14	24	34	44	54	64	74	84	94
5	15	25	35	45	55	65	75	85	95
6	16	26	36	46	56	66	76	86	96
7	17	27	37	47	57	67	77	87	97
8	18	28	38	48	58	68	78	88	98
9	19	29	39	49	59	69	79	89	99
10	20	30	40	50	60	70	80	90	100

S

shapes

2-dimensional   3-dimensional

shorter

The crayon is **shorter** than the pencil.

shortest

The paper clip is the **shortest**.

Show All Totals Method*

$$
\begin{array}{r}
25 \\
+\ 48 \\
\hline
60 \\
13 \\
\hline
73
\end{array}
$$

*A classroom research-based term developed for *Math Expressions*

side

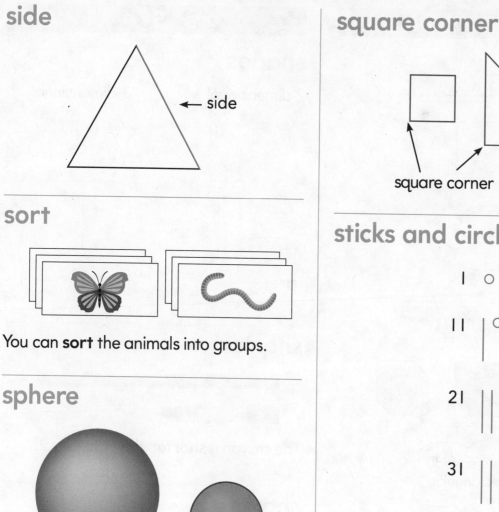

← side

sort

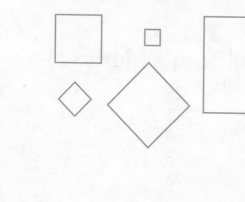

You can **sort** the animals into groups.

sphere

square

square corner

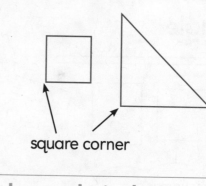

↑ ↑
square corner

sticks and circles*

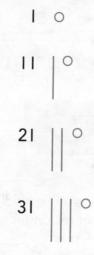

1	○
11	○
21	○
31	○

subtract

$8 - 3 = 5$

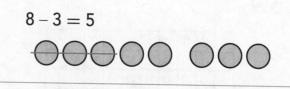

subtraction story problem

8 flies are on a log.
6 are eaten by a frog.
How many flies are left?

*A classroom research-based term developed for *Math Expressions*

switch the partners*

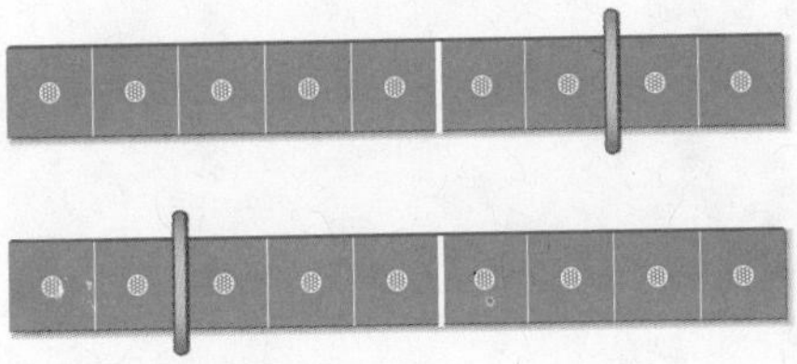

7 + 2

2 + 7

T

teen number

11 12 13 14 15 16 17 18 19

teen numbers

teen total*

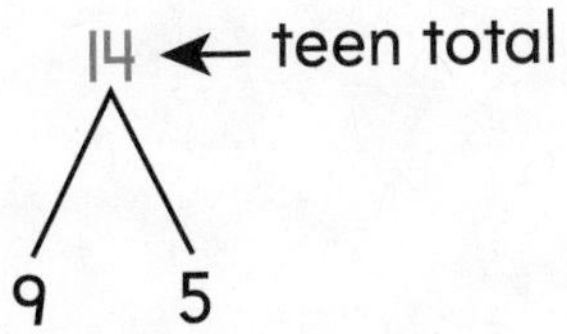

14 ← teen total

9   5

tens

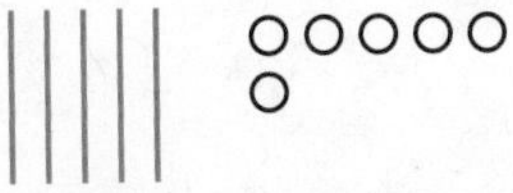

tens

56 has 5 **tens**.

total

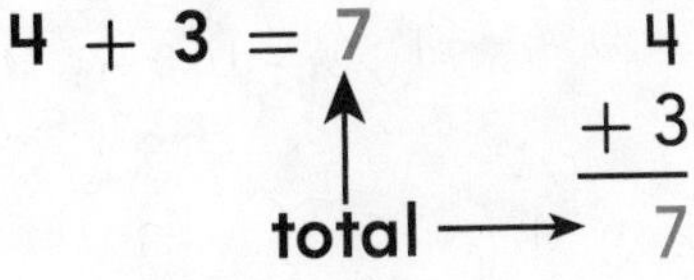

4 + 3 = 7   4
           ↑   + 3
       total → 7

trapezoid

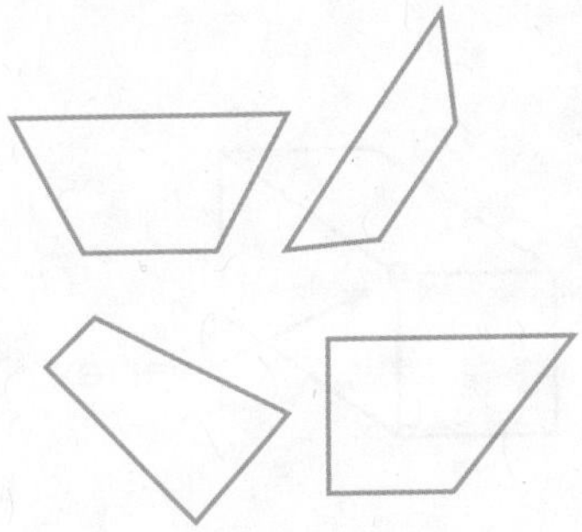

triangle

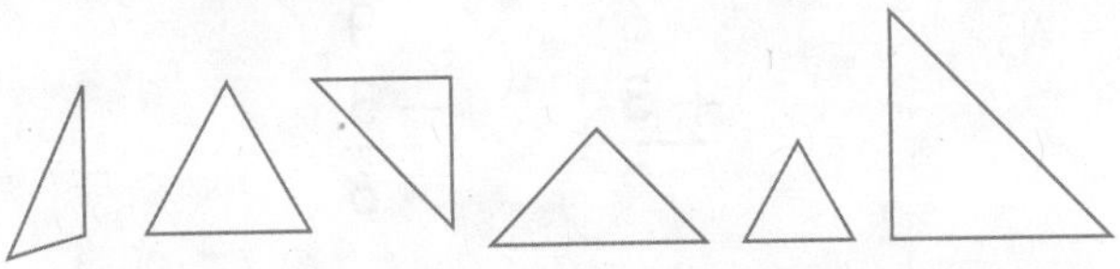

U

unknown partner*

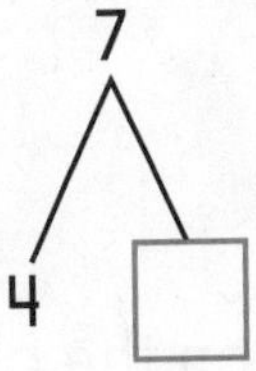

7

4   ☐   4 + ☐ = 7

unknown total*

☐

5 3   5 + 3 = ☐

*A classroom research-based term developed for *Math Expressions*

V

vertex

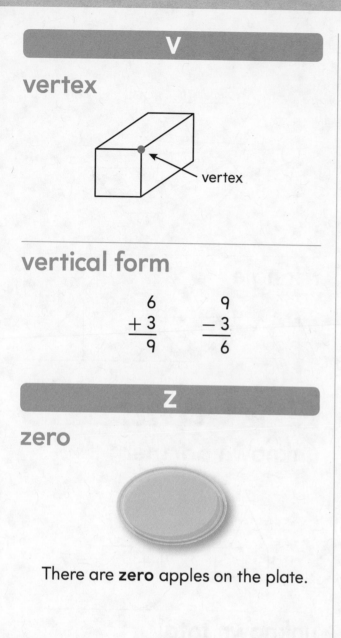

vertex

---

vertical form

$$\begin{array}{r} 6 \\ +\,3 \\ \hline 9 \end{array} \qquad \begin{array}{r} 9 \\ -\,3 \\ \hline 6 \end{array}$$

Z

zero

There are **zero** apples on the plate.

1.OA Operations and Algebraic Thinking

Represent and solve problems involving addition and subtraction.

1.OA.A.1	Use addition and subtraction within 20 to solve word problems involving situations of adding to, taking from, putting together, taking apart, and comparing, with unknowns in all positions, e.g., by using objects, drawings, and equations with a symbol for the unknown number to represent the problem.	Unit 1 Lessons 2, 3, 4, 5, 6, 7, 8; Unit 2 Lessons 1, 2, 3, 4, 6, 8, 10, 11, 12, 13, 14, 15, 16; Unit 3 Lessons 2, 3, 4, 5, 6, 7, 8, 9, 10, 11, 12; Unit 4 Lesson 5; Unit 5 Lessons 1, 2, 3, 4, 5, 11; Unit 6 Lessons 1, 2, 3, 4, 5, 6, 7, 8, 9
1.OA.A.2	Solve word problems that call for addition of three whole numbers whose sum is less than or equal to 20, e.g., by using objects, drawings, and equations with a symbol for the unknown number to represent the problem.	Unit 5 Lessons 6, 11; Unit 6 Lessons 1, 4, 5, 9

Understand and apply properties of operations and the relationship between addition and subtraction.

1.OA.B.3	Apply properties of operations as strategies to add and subtract.	Unit 1 Lessons 3, 4, 5, 6, 7, 8, 9; Unit 2 Lessons 7, 8, 9, 13; Unit 3 Lesson 5; Unit 4 Lessons 5, 10; Unit 5 Lessons 4, 6
1.OA.B.4	Understand subtraction as an unknown-addend problem.	Unit 3 Lessons 6, 7, 8, 9, 10, 12; Unit 5 Lessons 2, 5, 10

Add and subtract within 20.

1.OA.C.5	Relate counting to addition and subtraction (e.g., by counting on 2 to add 2).	Unit 1 Lessons 1, 2, 3, 4, 9; Unit 2 Lessons 5, 6, 7, 8, 9; Unit 3 Lessons 1, 3, 4, 6, 7, 11; Unit 4 Lessons 1, 4, 5, 7, 15, 16, 17; Unit 5 Lessons 1, 2, 4

■ **Major**   ■ **Supporting**   ■ **Additional**

| 1.OA.C.6 | Add and subtract within 20, demonstrating fluency for addition and subtraction within 10. Use strategies such as counting on; making ten (e.g., $8 + 6 = 8 + 2 + 4 = 10 + 4 = 14$); decomposing a number leading to a ten (e.g., $13 - 4 = 13 - 3 - 1 = 10 - 1 = 9$); using the relationship between addition and subtraction (e.g., knowing that $8 + 4 = 12$, one knows $12 - 8 = 4$); and creating equivalent but easier or known sums (e.g., adding $6 + 7$ by creating the known equivalent $6 + 6 + 1 = 12 + 1 = 13$). | Unit 1 Lessons 3, 4, 5, 6, 7, 8, 9; Unit 2 Lessons 1, 2, 3, 5, 6, 7, 8, 9, 10, 11, 12, 13, 14, 15, 16; Unit 3 Lessons 1, 3, 4, 5, 6, 7, 10, 11, 12; Unit 4 Lessons 4, 5, 6, 10, 15; Unit 5 Lessons 1, 2, 3, 4, 5, 10, 11; Unit 6 Lessons 3, 8; Unit 7 Lessons 5, 8, 13; Unit 8 Lesson 5 |

Work with addition and subtraction equations.

| 1.OA.D.7 | Understand the meaning of the equal sign, and determine if equations involving addition and subtraction are true or false. | Unit 2 Lessons 3, 4, 11, 12, 13, 16; Unit 3 Lesson 12; Unit 5 Lesson 11 |
| 1.OA.D.8 | Determine the unknown whole number in an addition or subtraction equation relating three whole numbers. | Unit 1 Lessons 3, 4, 5, 6, 7, 8; Unit 2 Lessons 5, 6, 7, 8, 9, 10, 12, 13, 14, 16; Unit 3 Lessons 3, 4, 5, 6, 7, 8, 9, 11, 12; Unit 4 Lessons 4, 5, 6, 10, 13, 14, 15, 16; Unit 5 Lessons 1, 2, 3, 4, 5, 10; Unit 6 Lessons 6, 7 |

1.NBT Number and Operations in Base Ten

Extend the counting sequence.

| 1.NBT.A.1 | Count to 120, starting at any number less than 120. In this range, read and write numerals and represent a number of objects with a written numeral. | Unit 4 Lessons 1, 2, 7, 8, 9, 10, 11, 15, 16, 18; Unit 5 Lessons 7, 8, 9; Unit 6 Lesson 6 |

■ **Major**   ■ **Supporting**   ■ **Additional**

Understand place value.

1.NBT.B.2	Understand that the two digits of a two-digit number represent amounts of tens and ones. Understand the following as special cases:	Unit 4 Lessons 1, 2, 3, 4, 7, 8, 9, 10, 11, 12, 13, 14, 16, 17, 18; Unit 5 Lessons 7, 8, 9; Unit 8 Lesson 1
1.NBT.B.2.a	a. 10 can be thought of as a bundle of ten ones — called a "ten."	Unit 4 Lessons 1, 2, 3, 4, 9, 10, 16, 18; Unit 5 Lessons 8, 10; Unit 8 Lesson 1
1.NBT.B.2.b	b. The numbers from 11 to 19 are composed of a ten and one, two, three, four, five, six, seven, eight, or nine ones.	Unit 4 Lessons 2, 3, 4, 5, 8, 10; Unit 5 Lesson 8
1.NBT.B.2.c	c. The numbers 10, 20, 30, 40, 50, 60, 70, 80, 90 refer to one, two, three, four, five, six, seven, eight, or nine tens (and 0 ones).	Unit 4 Lessons 1, 7, 8, 9, 13, 14, 18; Unit 5 Lesson 10; Unit 8 Lesson 1
1.NBT.B.3	Compare two two-digit numbers based on meanings of the tens and ones digits, recording the results of comparisons with the symbols >, =, and <.	Unit 4 Lessons 3, 12, 16, 18; Unit 8 Lesson 6

Use place value understanding and properties of operations to add and subtract.

1.NBT.C.4	Add within 100, including adding a two-digit number and a one-digit number, and adding a two-digit number and a multiple of 10, using concrete models or drawings and strategies based on place value, properties of operations, and/or the relationship between addition and subtraction; relate the strategy to a written method and explain the reasoning used. Understand that in adding two-digit numbers, one adds tens and tens, ones and ones; and sometimes it is necessary to compose a ten.	Unit 4 Lessons 9, 10, 11, 13, 14, 15, 16, 17, 18; Unit 5 Lessons 9, 10, 11; Unit 8 Lessons 1, 2, 3, 4, 5, 6
1.NBT.C.5	Given a two-digit number, mentally find 10 more or 10 less than the number, without having to count; explain the reasoning used.	Unit 5 Lessons 8, 9
1.NBT.C.6	Subtract multiples of 10 in the range 10–90 from multiples of 10 in the range 10–90 (positive or zero differences), using concrete models or drawings and strategies based on place value, properties of operations, and/or the relationship between addition and subtraction; relate the strategy to a written method and explain the reasoning used.	Unit 5 Lessons 9, 10, 11; Unit 8 Lesson 6

Common Core State Standards for Mathematical Content

1.MD Measurement and Data

Measure lengths indirectly and by iterating length units.

1.MD.A.1	Order three objects by length; compare the lengths of two objects indirectly by using a third object.	Unit 7 Lessons 12, 14
1.MD.A.2	Express the length of an object as a whole number of length units, by laying multiple copies of a shorter object (the length unit) end to end; understand that the length measurement of an object is the number of same-size length units that span it with no gaps or overlaps.	Unit 7 Lessons 13, 14

Tell and write time.

1.MD.B.3	Tell and write time in hours and half-hours using analog and digital clocks.	Unit 7 Lessons 1, 2, 3, 4, 5, 14

Represent and interpret data.

1.MD.C.4	Organize, represent, and interpret data with up to three categories; ask and answer questions about the total number of data points, how many in each category, and how many more or less are in one category than in another.	Unit 6 Lessons 1, 2, 3, 4, 5, 9

1.G Geometry

Reason with shapes and their attributes.

1.G.A.1	Distinguish between defining attributes (e.g., triangles are closed and three-sided) versus non-defining attributes (e.g., color, orientation, overall size); build and draw shapes to possess defining attributes.	Unit 7 Lessons 6, 7, 8, 9, 10
1.G.A.2	Compose two-dimensional shapes (rectangles, squares, trapezoids, triangles, half-circles, and quarter-circles) or three-dimensional shapes (cubes, right rectangular prisms, right circular cones, and right circular cylinders) to create a composite shape, and compose new shapes from the composite shape.	Unit 7 Lessons 9, 10, 11
1.G.A.3	Partition circles and rectangles into two and four equal shares, describe the shares using the words *halves*, *fourths*, and *quarters*, and use the phrases *half of, fourth of,* and *quarter of*. Describe the whole as two of, or four of the shares. Understand for these examples that decomposing into more equal shares creates smaller shares.	Unit 7 Lessons 8, 9, 14

■ Major ■ Supporting ■ Additional

© Houghton Mifflin Harcourt Publishing Company

MP1 Make sense of problems and persevere in solving them.

Mathematically proficient students start by explaining to themselves the meaning of a problem and looking for entry points to its solution. They analyze givens, constraints, relationships, and goals. They make conjectures about the form and meaning of the solution and plan a solution pathway rather than simply jumping into a solution attempt. They consider analogous problems, and try special cases and simpler forms of the original problem in order to gain insight into its solution. They monitor and evaluate their progress and change course if necessary. Older students might, depending on the context of the problem, transform algebraic expressions or change the viewing window on their graphing calculator to get the information they need. Mathematically proficient students can explain correspondences between equations, verbal descriptions, tables, and graphs or draw diagrams of important features and relationships, graph data, and search for regularity or trends. Younger students might rely on using concrete objects or pictures to help conceptualize and solve a problem. Mathematically proficient students check their answers to problems using a different method, and they continually ask themselves, "Does this make sense?" They can understand the approaches of others to solving complex problems and identify correspondences between different approaches.

Unit 1 Lessons 2, 3, 4, 6, 8, 9
Unit 2 Lessons 1, 2, 3, 4, 6, 7, 8, 9, 10, 13, 14, 16
Unit 3 Lessons 1, 2, 3, 4, 6, 7, 8, 9, 10, 11, 12
Unit 4 Lessons 2, 5, 10, 18
Unit 5 Lessons 1, 2, 3, 4, 5, 6, 11
Unit 6 Lessons 1, 2, 4, 6, 7, 8, 9
Unit 7 Lessons 8, 14
Unit 8 Lessons 1, 3, 4, 6

MP2 Reason abstractly and quantitatively.

Mathematically proficient students make sense of quantities and their relationships in problem situations. They bring two complementary abilities to bear on problems involving quantitative relationships: the ability to *decontextualize*—to abstract a given situation and represent it symbolically and manipulate the representing symbols as if they have a life of their own, without necessarily attending to their referents— and the ability to *contextualize*, to pause as needed during the manipulation process in order to probe into the referents for the symbols involved. Quantitative reasoning entails habits of creating a coherent representation of the problem at hand; considering the units involved; attending to the meaning of quantities, not just how to compute them; and knowing and flexibly using different properties of operations and objects.

Unit 1 Lessons 3, 4, 5, 6, 7, 8, 9
Unit 2 Lessons 1, 2, 3, 4, 6, 10, 11, 12, 13, 15, 16
Unit 3 Lessons 3, 5, 6, 12
Unit 4 Lessons 1, 3, 4, 6, 7, 8, 9, 10, 11, 12, 14, 15, 16, 17, 18
Unit 5 Lessons 1, 2, 3, 4, 5, 9, 10, 11
Unit 6 Lessons 1, 2, 3, 5, 6, 8, 9
Unit 7 Lessons 8, 9, 14
Unit 8 Lessons 1, 2, 3, 4, 5, 6

MP3 Construct viable arguments and critique the reasoning of others.

Mathematically proficient students understand and use stated assumptions, definitions, and previously established results in constructing arguments. They make conjectures and build a logical progression of statements to explore the truth of their conjectures. They are able to analyze situations by breaking them into cases, and can recognize and use counterexamples. They justify their conclusions, communicate them to others, and respond to the arguments of others. They reason inductively about data, making plausible arguments that take into account the context from which the data arose. Mathematically proficient students are also able to compare the effectiveness of two plausible arguments, distinguish correct logic or reasoning from that which is flawed, and—if there is a flaw in an argument—explain what it is. Elementary students can construct arguments using concrete referents such as objects, drawings, diagrams, and actions. Such arguments can make sense and be correct, even though they are not generalized or made formal until later grades. Later, students learn to determine domains to which an argument applies. Students at all grades can listen or read the arguments of others, decide whether they make sense, and ask useful questions to clarify or improve the arguments.

Unit 1 Lessons 1, 2, 3, 4, 5, 6, 7, 8, 9
Unit 2 Lessons 1, 2, 3, 4, 6, 7, 8, 9, 10, 11, 12, 13, 14, 16
Unit 3 Lessons 2, 3, 4, 5, 6, 7, 8, 9, 10, 11, 12
Unit 4 Lessons 1, 2, 3, 4, 5, 6, 7, 8, 9, 10, 11, 12, 13, 14, 15, 16, 17, 18
Unit 5 Lessons 1, 2, 3, 4, 5, 6, 7, 8, 9, 10, 11
Unit 6 Lessons 1, 2, 3, 4, 5, 6, 7, 8, 9
Unit 7 Lessons 1, 2, 3, 4, 5, 6, 7, 8, 9, 10, 11, 12, 13, 14
Unit 8 Lessons 1, 2, 3, 4, 5, 6

MP4 Model with mathematics.

Mathematically proficient students can apply the mathematics they know to solve problems arising in everyday life, society, and the workplace. In early grades, this might be as simple as writing an addition equation to describe a situation. In middle grades, a student might apply proportional reasoning to plan a school event or analyze a problem in the community. By high school, a student might use geometry to solve a design problem or use a function to describe how one quantity of interest depends on another. Mathematically proficient students who can apply what they know are comfortable making assumptions and approximations to simplify a complicated situation, realizing that these may need revision later. They are able to identify important quantities in a practical situation and map their relationships using such tools as diagrams, two-way tables, graphs, flowcharts and formulas. They can analyze those relationships mathematically to draw conclusions. They routinely interpret their mathematical results in the context of the situation and reflect on whether the results make sense, possibly improving the model if it has not served its purpose.

Unit 1 Lessons 2, 3, 9
Unit 2 Lessons 1, 2, 10, 13, 16
Unit 3 Lessons 1, 2, 5, 6, 7, 8, 9, 10, 11, 12
Unit 4 Lessons 2, 3, 5, 10, 18
Unit 5 Lessons 1, 2, 3, 4, 6, 11
Unit 6 Lessons 2, 3, 4, 5, 6, 7, 8, 9
Unit 7 Lessons 3, 8, 14
Unit 8 Lessons 1, 2, 3, 6

MP5 Use appropriate tools strategically.

Mathematically proficient students consider the available tools when solving a mathematical problem. These tools might include pencil and paper, concrete models, a ruler, a protractor, a calculator, a spreadsheet, a computer algebra system, a statistical package, or dynamic geometry software. Proficient students are sufficiently familiar with tools appropriate for their grade or course to make sound decisions about when each of these tools might be helpful, recognizing both the insight to be gained and their limitations. For example, mathematically proficient high school students analyze graphs of functions and solutions generated using a graphing calculator. They detect possible errors by strategically using estimation and other mathematical knowledge. When making mathematical models, they know that technology can enable them to visualize the results of varying assumptions, explore consequences, and compare predictions with data. Mathematically proficient students at various grade levels are able to identify relevant external mathematical resources, such as digital content located on a website, and use them to pose or solve problems. They are able to use technological tools to explore and deepen their understanding of concepts.

Unit 1 Lessons 1, 2, 3, 4, 5, 6, 7, 8, 9
Unit 2 Lessons 5, 6, 8, 16
Unit 3 Lessons 1, 2, 3, 4, 7, 11, 12
Unit 4 Lessons 1, 2, 3, 4, 5, 6, 7, 8, 9, 10, 11, 12, 13, 14, 16, 17, 18
Unit 5 Lessons 1, 2, 6, 8, 9, 10, 11
Unit 6 Lessons 3, 4, 5, 9
Unit 7 Lessons 1, 2, 5, 6, 7, 8, 9, 10, 11, 12, 13, 14
Unit 8 Lessons 2, 3, 6

MP6 Attend to precision.

Mathematically proficient students try to communicate precisely to others. They try to use clear definitions in discussion with others and in their own reasoning. They state the meaning of the symbols they choose, including using the equal sign consistently and appropriately. They are careful about specifying units of measure, and labeling axes to clarify the correspondence with quantities in a problem. They calculate accurately and efficiently, express numerical answers with a degree of precision appropriate for the problem context. In the elementary grades, students give carefully formulated explanations to each other. By the time they reach high school they have learned to examine claims and make explicit use of definitions.

Unit 1 Lessons 1, 2, 3, 4, 5, 6, 7, 8, 9
Unit 2 Lessons 1, 3, 4, 5, 6, 7, 8, 9, 10, 11, 12, 13, 14, 15, 16
Unit 3 Lessons 1, 2, 3, 4, 5, 6, 7, 8, 9, 10, 11, 12
Unit 4 Lessons 1, 2, 3, 4, 5, 6, 7, 8, 9, 10, 11, 12, 13, 14, 15, 16, 17, 18
Unit 5 Lessons 1, 2, 3, 4, 5, 6, 7, 8, 9, 10, 11
Unit 6 Lessons 1, 2, 3, 4, 5, 6, 7, 8, 9
Unit 7 Lessons 1, 2, 3, 4, 5, 6, 7, 8, 9, 10, 11, 12, 13, 14
Unit 8 Lessons 1, 2, 3, 4, 5, 6

Common Core State Standards for Mathematical Practice

MP7 Look for and make use of structure.

Mathematically proficient students look closely to discern a pattern or structure. Young students, for example, might notice that three and seven more is the same amount as seven and three more, or they may sort a collection of shapes according to how many sides the shapes have. Later, students will see 7×8 equals the well remembered $7 \times 5 + 7 \times 3$, in preparation for learning about the distributive property. In the expression $x^2 + 9x + 14$, older students can see the 14 as 2×7 and the 9 as $2 + 7$. They recognize the significance of an existing line in a geometric figure and can use the strategy of drawing an auxiliary line for solving problems. They also can step back for an overview and shift perspective. They can see complicated things, such as some algebraic expressions, as single objects or as being composed of several objects. For example, they can see $5 - 3(x - y)^2$ as 5 minus a positive number times a square and use that to realize that its value cannot be more than 5 for any real numbers x and y.

Unit 1 Lessons 1, 2, 3, 4, 5, 6, 7, 8, 9
Unit 2 Lessons 13, 14, 16
Unit 3 Lessons 1, 3, 9, 12
Unit 4 Lessons 1, 2, 3, 5, 6, 7, 8, 9, 10, 13, 17, 18
Unit 5 Lessons 1, 2, 3, 5, 6, 7, 8, 9, 10, 11
Unit 6 Lessons 6, 8, 9
Unit 7 Lessons 1, 2, 3, 4, 5, 6, 7, 9, 10, 11, 14
Unit 8 Lessons 2, 6

MP8 Look for and express regularity in repeated reasoning.

Mathematically proficient students notice if calculations are repeated, and look both for general methods and for shortcuts. Upper elementary students might notice when dividing 25 by 11 that they are repeating the same calculations over and over again, and conclude they have a repeating decimal. By paying attention to the calculation of slope as they repeatedly check whether points are on the line through (1, 2) with slope 3, middle school students might abstract the equation $(y - 2)/(x - 1) = 3$. Noticing the regularity in the way terms cancel when expanding $(x - 1)(x + 1)$, $(x - 1)(x^2 + x + 1)$, and $(x - 1)(x^3 + x^2 + x + 1)$ might lead them to the general formula for the sum of a geometric series. As they work to solve a problem, mathematically proficient students maintain oversight of the process, while attending to the details. They continually evaluate the reasonableness of their intermediate results.

Unit 1 Lessons 1, 2, 3, 4, 5, 6, 7, 8, 9
Unit 2 Lessons 6, 7, 8, 11, 14, 16
Unit 3 Lessons 8, 9, 12
Unit 4 Lessons 1, 2, 5, 6, 7, 9, 10, 12, 13, 14, 15, 17, 18
Unit 5 Lessons 1, 2, 4, 5, 6, 7, 8, 9, 10, 11
Unit 6 Lessons 1, 6, 7, 9
Unit 7 Lessons 3, 6, 7, 8, 9, 10, 12, 14
Unit 8 Lessons 1, 2, 3, 4, 6

A

Addends
three addends, 221–222

Addition
within 10, 20, 21–22, 23, 26, 27–28, 29, 43–50, 55–60, 65–66, 81–86, 97–98, 99–102, 107–108, 123–128, 131, 154
within 20, 153–154, 159–162, 207–208, 217–218, 219, 235–236
within 100. *See* Two-digit numbers.
add tens, 232–233
Associative Property, 255, 337–338
Commutative Property, 23, 25, 27, 235–236
equation
determine the unknown whole number in, 99–102, 126–127, 235–236
represent an unknown in, 81, 97–98, 99–101, 123–124, 184, 207, 217–218
true and false, 50
writing, 145, 147, 148
Fluency Check, 52, 70, 112, 180, 194, 238, 260, 296, 326, 348
fluency practice, 102, 172, 186, 234, 254, 260, 294, 322, 344
model
comparison bars, 261–262, 263
counting blocks, 7
drawings
circle, 8, 11–13, 19, 23, 25, 27, 29, 45–49, 55–56
ten-stick and circles, 151–152, 169–170, 181–182
equations, 20, 47–48, 99–101, 159, 207, 217, 220, 235–236
fingers, 7
Math Mountains, 19, 21, 23, 25, 27, 44, 97–98, 110, 123–124, 132, 263

plus sign, 19, 43–44
relate to subtraction, 81, 123–124
situation and solution equations, 119–120, 124–128, 263
story problems. *See also* Problem Types.
solve with drawings, 49, 99–101, 107–108, 125–128, 131, 151
solve with equations, 81, 83–86, 147, 148, 235–236, 263
solve with objects, 99, 131, 221–222
with three addends, 235
story writing, 12, 14
strategies
counting on, 55–60, 65–66, 101, 188
doubles, 22, 26, 30, 161–162
doubles minus one, 161
doubles minus two, 161
doubles plus one, 161
doubles plus two, 161
make a ten, 153–154, 159
patterns, 20, 22, 24, 26, 28, 30
three addends, 235, 255
vertical form, 82–84
Zero Property, 20, 22, 26, 30

Algebra
determine the unknown whole number in an equation, 99–102, 109, 117, 126,127, 215–216, 217–218, 219–220, 235–236
inverse operations, addition and subtraction, 81, 123–124, 263
modeling equations, 21, 47–48, 67–68 99–100, 123–124, 159, 207, 215–216, 217, 220, 221–222, 235–236
properties
Associative Property, 221–222, 235–236, 255, 337–338

Commutative Property, 23, 25, 27, 29

Zero Property, 20, 22, 26, 30

situation and solution equations, 123–124, 263

symbols

equal (=), 47–48, 152, 188

inequality (<, >), 177–178, 188

minus (–), 71–78

plus (+), 15–16, 43–44

unknown addends, 97–102, 107–108, 124, 154, 207–208, 215

writing an equation, 47–48, 73–76, 109, 117, 133–134, 159, 220

writing a related equation, 81–82, 123–124, 263

Assessment

Fluency Check, 52, 70, 80, 88, 112, 122, 136, 164, 180, 194, 224, 238, 260, 270, 296, 318, 326, 348

Formative Assessment

Performance Task, 38–39, 93–94, 141–142, 199–200, 243–244, 275–276, 331–332, 353–354

Unit Review/Test, 34–37, 89–92, 137–140, 195–198, 239–242, 271–274, 327–330, 349–352

Quick Quiz, 13, 33, 51, 69, 79, 87, 111, 121, 135, 163, 179, 193, 223, 237, 259, 269, 295, 317, 325, 347

Strategy Check, 14, 34

Attributes. *See* **Geometry; Sorting and classifying.**

B

Break-aparts

Break-Apart Stick, 15, 17, 19, 21

C

Circle, 303–304

Circle drawings, 21, 23, 27, 29, 45–49, 73–77, 123–124, 151–152

Clock. *See also* **Time.**

analog, 281–282, 287–295

digital, 282, 291–292, 293–294

hour hand, 282–283, 285–286, 291–294

minute hand, 282–283, 291–294

for "Our Busy Day" Book, 287–288

Columns, 229–231

Common Core Standards, S17–S24

Commutative Property, 23. *See also* **Addition.**

Compare. *See* **Length; Numbers.**

Comparison bars, 261–266

Cone, 313–314, 315–316

Corners, 301, 303–304, 310

Counting

to 10, 31

count on, 55–60, 68–69, 101, 188

One Hundred Twenty Grid, 229–231

number words, 167–168

read and write numerals, 31, 167–168, 189–190, 229–230

represent a set with a written numeral, 43–44, 145, 148, 249–250

represent a set with drawings, 249–252

tens and ones, 145–148, 165–166, 168, 189–190, 225–226

Cube, 313–314, 315–316

Cylinder, 313–314, 315–316

D

Data
ask and answer questions, 247, 249–250, 256, 267
comparison bars, 261–268
discuss, 255
interpret, 249–250, 253–258, 267
matching drawings, 256, 267–268
more and fewer, 249–254, 256–258
organize, 247, 249–250, 256–257, 258, 267
represent, 249–250, 256–257, 258
three categories, 255–258
two categories, 247, 249–254, 267

Doubles. *See* **Addition; Numbers.**

Drawing
addition and subtraction, 8
explaining equations, 50
lines, 320
more to count on, 65
shapes, 301, 303, 304

E

Edges, 313–314

Equal shares
fourths, 307–308, 323
halves, 305–307, 323
manipulatives, 305–306
partition into, 307–308
quarters, 307–308, 323

Equations. *See* **Algebra.**

F

Faces, 313–314

Family Letter, 1–4, 15–18, 41–42, 53–54, 95–96, 143–144, 149–150,
201–202, 245–246, 277–280, 333–334

Five-groups, 8, 11–14

Fluency
Check, 52, 70, 80, 88, 112, 122, 136, 164, 180, 194, 224, 238, 260, 270, 296, 318, 326, 348
Path to Fluency, 52, 70, 80, 88, 102, 112, 114, 122, 128, 135, 162, 164, 172, 180, 186, 194, 218, 224, 234, 238, 254, 260, 266, 270, 294, 296, 308, 322, 326, 344, 348

Focus on Mathematical Practices, 31, 85–86, 133–134, 191–192, 235–236, 267–268, 323–324, 345–346

G

Geometry. *See also* **Equal shares.**
attributes
closed, 303–304
corners, 301, 303–304, 310
square corners, 301, 304, 310
edges, 313–314
faces, 313–314
sides, 301, 303–304, 310
vertices, 313–314
three-dimensional shapes, 313–314, 315–316
attributes, 313–314
build, 316
compose, 315–316
compose new shapes from the composite shape, 315–316
cone, 313–314, 315–316
cube, 313–314, 315–316
cylinder, 313–314, 315–316
rectangular prism, 313–314, 315–316
sphere, 313–314, 315

two-dimensional shapes
  build and draw, 301, 303–304, 310
  circle, 303–304
  compose, 310, 312
    compose new shapes from the
      composite shape, 312
  rectangle, 301–302
  sort, 301, 302
  square, 301–302, 310
  triangle, 303–304, 310

Groups
  of 5, 11
  5-groups, 8, 11–14
  of 6, 11
  of 7, 11
  of 8, 11
  of 9, 11
  of 10, 11
  ten-groups, 225–226

H

Hundred Grid, 229–231

I

Inch Grid, 309

Inverse relationship
  addition, 81, 123–124
  subtraction, 81, 123–124

L

Length
  iterate, 321–322, 324
  order, 319–320, 324
  units, 321–322, 324

M

Make-a-Ten
  strategy, 154, 159, 213–214

Make-a-Ten Cards, 155–158, 203–206, 209–212

Manipulatives
  base ten blocks, 145, 146, 148, 349
  Break-Apart Sticks, 19, 21
  clocks for "Our Busy Day" Book, 287–288
  connecting cubes, 17, 221
  Count-On Cards, 61–62, 103–104, 115–116
  Hundred Grid, 229–231
  Make-a-Ten Cards, 155–158, 203–206, 209–212
  MathBoard materials, 85–86, 236, 267–268, 337–338, 341
  Number Cards, 5–6, 9–10
  Number Quilt, 63–64, 105–106, 129–130
  for representing data, 247–248
  Sandwich Sheet, 187
  Secret Code Cards, 173–174
  Stair Steps, 5–6, 17, 19, 21
  Student Clock, 283–284
  Triangle Grid, 311
  Two-Dimensional Shape Set, 297–300, 312

Math Mountains, 19, 21, 23, 25, 27, 44, 97–98, 110, 119, 123–124, 132, 263

Measurement
  length
    iterate, 321–322, 324
    order, 319–320, 324
    units, 321–322, 324

time
  analog clock, 282–283, 285–286, 289–294
  digital clock, 285, 290–294
  half-hour, 291–292, 293–294
  hour, 285–286, 289–290, 294

N

New Group Above method, 337–338, 341

New Group Below method, 337–338, 341

Number-Bond diagram. See Math Mountains.

Numbers
  5-groups, 8, 11–14
  to 10, 19–20, 21–22, 23–24, 26, 27–28, 31
  to 100, 151–152, 167–168, 169–170, 175–176, 191–192, 231
  to 120, 229–230
  compare, 150, 188, 192
  decade, 168
  doubles, 22, 26, 161–162
  finding on a grid, 229–230
  number words, 167–168
  read and write, 31, 167–168, 191–192, 229–230
  represent, 19, 21, 23, 25, 27, 29, 151–152, 165–166, 169, 171, 175–176, 191–192, 249–252, 254
  teen, 151–154, 159–162, 161–162, 167–168, 207–208, 213–214, 215–216, 217–218, 219–220
  ten-groups, 225–226
  ten more and ten less, 229–230
  two-digit, 151–152, 165–166, 167–168, 175–176
  zero, 20, 22, 26, 30

P

Partners. See also Break-Aparts; Math Mountains.
  of 2, 19, 22, 24, 28, 30
  of 3, 19, 22, 24, 26, 28, 30
  of 4, 19, 22, 24, 26, 28, 30
  of 5, 2, 4, 19, 22, 24, 26, 28, 30
  of 6, 21–22, 24, 26, 28, 30
  of 7, 23–24, 26, 28, 30
  of 8, 25–26, 28, 30
  of 9, 27–28, 30, 33
  of 10, 29–30, 32
  finding the unknown, 294, 296
  patterns in, 22, 24, 26, 28, 30
  switch, 23, 25, 27, 55–60, 221. See also Addition.
  train, 21, 23, 25, 27
  unknown, 97–98, 99–100, 123–124, 207
  zero as a partner, 20, 22, 26, 30

Patterns
  with doubles, 30
  in partners, 22, 24, 26, 28, 29, 30
  solving equations with, 20, 22, 24, 26, 28
  with zero, 30

Performance Task, 38–39, 93–94, 141–142, 199–200, 243–244, 275–276, 331–332, 353–354

Place value, 160, 169–170, 175–176, 182, 187, 191–192
  addition
    add with place value, 191–192, 235–236, 337–343
    New Group Above method, 337–343
    New Group Below method, 337–343
    Show All Totals method, 341

Index

Problem solving. *See* **Addition; Problem Types; Subtraction.**

Problem Types, S1–S3
Add To with Change Unknown, 97–102, 107–108, 119–120, 123–124, 125–126, 131, 208, 219
Add To with Result Unknown, 81, 124–126
Add To with Start Unknown, 125–126, 127–128, 208, 219, 236
Compare with Bigger Unknown, 263, 265–266
Compare with Difference Unknown, 261–262, 264, 265–266, 268
Compare with Smaller Unknown, 263–264, 265–266, 268
Put Together/Take Apart with Addend Unknown, 97–102, 107–108, 119–120, 123–124, 208, 215
Put Together/Take Apart with Both Addends Unknown, 100, 215
Put Together/Take Apart with Total Unknown, 81, 85, 128, 208, 219–220, 216
Take From with Change Unknown, 125, 128, 216
Take From with Result Unknown, 81, 107–108, 119, 128, 216
Take From with Start Unknown, 124, 128, 131, 216, 220, 236

Properties
Associative (addition), 221–222, 235–236, 337–338
Commutative (addition), 23, 25, 27
Zero (addition), 20, 22, 26, 30

Puzzled Penguin, 72, 102, 153, 178, 184, 220, 234, 253, 286, 292, 344

Q

Quick Quiz, 13, 33, 51, 69, 79, 87, 111, 121, 135, 163, 179, 193, 223, 237, 259, 269, 295, 317, 325, 347

R

Real world problems. *See* **Problem Types.**

Rectangle, 301–302

Rectangular prism, 313–314, 315–316

Rows, 229–231

S

Show All Totals Method, 341

Sides, 301, 303–304

Sorting and classifying
by attribute, 301, 314
by category, 247, 249–255
by shape, 302

Sphere, 313–314, 315

Square, 301

Strategy Check, 14, 34

Student Clock, 283–284

Subtraction
within 10, 30, 71–78, 81–82, 83–86, 107–108, 117–120, 124–128, 133–134
within 20, 213–214, 215–216, 217–218, 219–220, 236
determine the unknown whole number, 113, 119, 124–128, 132–133, 215–216, 220, 235–236
equation, 71–78, 213–214

Fluency Check, 80, 88, 122, 136, 164, 224, 238, 270, 318

fluency practice, 80, 88, 114, 122, 128, 135, 162, 164, 218, 234, 238, 266, 308

minus sign, 71–78

model
  comparison bars, 261–266
  drawings
    circle, 73–77, 81
    equations, 124, 128, 215–216, 236
    Math Mountains, 119, 124, 263
  multiples of ten, 313–314
  relate to addition, 81, 123–124
  represent an unknown in, 63, 124–128
  situation and solution equations, 123–124, 263
  story problems. *See also* Problem Types.
    solve with comparison bars, 264–265
    solve with drawings, 77, 107–108, 117, 125–128
    solve with equations, 71–72, 77, 81, 83–86, 113–114, 124, 133
    solve with objects, 215–216, 235
    writing, 134
  strategies
    decompose a number leading to a ten, 214
    doubles, 22, 26
    make a ten, 213–214
    patterns, 20, 22, 24, 26, 30
    relate addition and subtraction, 81, 123–124, 127
    understand subtraction as an unknown addend problem, 81, 119, 124, 131, 133–134
  subtract tens, 232–234
  true and false, 78
  vertical form, 82–84

Symbols
  equal (=), 47–48, 152, 188
  inequality (<, >), 177–178, 188
  minus (–), 71–78
  plus (+), 20–21, 43–44

T

Tape diagrams. *See* **Comparison bars.**

Teen Numbers, 151–154, 159–162, 167–168, 207–208, 215–216, 217–218, 219–220

Ten-groups, 225–226

Three-dimensional shapes. *See* **Geometry.**

Time
  analog clock, 281–282, 285–286, 289–290, 291–292, 293–294
  digital clock, 285, 289–290, 291–292, 293–294
  half-hour, 291–292, 293–294
  hour, 285–286, 289–290, 294

Triangle, 303–304

Two-digit numbers, 151–152, 167–168, 191
  10 less, 229–230
  10 more, 144–145, 229–230
  addition
    2-digit plus 1-digit, 183–184, 185, 188, 191–192, 343, 347
    2-digit plus 2-digit, 181–184, 187, 335–336, 337–343, 345–346, 347, 349–352
    2-digit plus a multiple of ten, 232–234, 336, 347
    add with drawings, 335–336
    add with place value, 191–192, 235–236, 337–343
      New Group Above method, 337–343

New Group Below method, 337–343

Show All Totals method, 341

add with properties, 337–338

compose a ten, 185, 188, 335–336, 337–343, 345–346, 347, 349–352

counting on, 185, 188

relate addition and subtraction, 232

of tens, 229–232

add with concrete models, 191–192

subtraction

relate addition and subtraction, 232

subtract with models, 236

subtract with place value, 236

of tens, 229–230, 232

Two-dimensional shapes. *See* Geometry; Manipulatives.

Two-Dimensional Shape Set, 297–300, 312

U

Unit Review/Test, 34–37, 89–92, 137–140, 195–198, 239–242, 271–274, 327–330, 349–352

V

Vocabulary Cards, 4A–4F, 42A–42F, 96A–96F, 144A–144F, 202A–202F, 246A–246F, 280A–280F, 334A–334F

Z

Zero. *See also* Numbers.

add zero, 20, 22, 26, 30

patterns with, 30

property of, 20, 22, 26, 30

subtract zero, 20, 22, 26, 30

Zero Property, 20, 22, 26, 30

Illustrator: Josh Brill

Did you ever try to use shapes to draw animals like the frog on the cover?

Over the last 10 years Josh has been using geometric shapes to design his animals. His aim is to keep the animal drawings simple and use color to make them appealing.

Add some color to the frog Josh drew. Then try drawing a cat or dog or some other animal using the shapes below.

Shape Toolbox